a maddy laine handbook

Christmas Feltings

Create holiday decorations and gift ideas
from felted handknitting

Maddy Cranley

Penguin Lane Press
Montreal

Published By:

Penguin Lane Press
Suite 401, 3445 Ridgewood Avenue
Montreal, Quebec, Canada
H3V 1B7

Other Books by Maddy Cranley:
Fulling Around With Felting

Canadian Cataloguing in Publication Data

Cranley, Maddy, 1948-
    Christmas feltings
    (A Maddy Laine handbook)
    Includes index.
    ISBN 0-9681448-2-9
    1. Christmas decorations. 2. Felt work. 3. Felting.
I. Title. II. Series: Cranley, Maddy, 1948- A Maddy Laine
handbook.
TT849.5.C73 1997   746.9   C97-900468-3

Every effort has been made to ensure that all information in this book is accurate. However, due to differing conditions, tools and individual skills, the publisher cannot be responsible for any injuries, losses, or other damages which may result from the use of the information in this book.

Printed in Canada

First Edition: August, 1997

Table of Contents

Introduction

Christmas comes along just at the right time of the year. In the shorter and darker days of the winter season, we really can appreciate some distraction and difference in our daily routines to make this one day stand out from the rest. For the crafters among us, Christmas gives us a reason to undertake a creative project and a deadline within which to complete it. The holiday decorations and gift ideas in this book, as in my previous book "Fulling Around With Felting", will find their start in handknitting, which is felted and embellished. Some of the items are for keeping in your own Christmas collections of holiday decorations. Other ideas are for giving - a lovable felted teddy bear, a door hanging crafted from felted cutouts or perhaps a unique felted gift bag to dress up a Christmas food specialty from your kitchen.

When the Christmas season draws near, one of my favorite days is to bring out the stored boxes of Christmas decorations and spend a few hours opening and unwrapping decorations that have been paid no mind since last year. It's as if you see these items for the first time, even though some have been in and out of those same boxes year after year. Some of the decorations, which I never seem to use, still remain in that box to be taken out and remind me of another memory. Funny enough, I have a felt decoration that I bought many years ago at a bazaar in San Francisco. I never use it (it's a light switch cover!), but every year it is unpacked, the memory is remembered, and it is placed back in the box to be preserved for next year's unwrapping. Each year, I try to add something new to my Christmas decoration collection. Like other trends in our fast-paced world, some of the items that are old become new again and seem to find their place among this year's holiday decorating plans.

Among the projects in this book, you will find items that are both practical and decorative. Felted stockings hung at a fireplace never seem to go out of style. This year try fashioning your Christmas stockings in different colors and styles to spruce up this age-old tradition. Maybe it's time to make a tree skirt to replace the same unfinished length of fabric that appears under the tree year after year. Let your neighbors know how creative you are and hang a colorful door banner that is both warm and welcoming. Don't limit yourself to the traditional Christmas green and red. Mix and match hues that cover the full spectrum of red and green, perhaps combining khaki green and rose or pear with claret. Add touches of silver and gold to make your holiday color scheme sparkle and shine.

For the convenience of those who did not read the first book, I have repeated basic information in regards to handknitting and felting techniques that are required to complete the projects in this book. For those who did enjoy the previous book, you will find new and added information in regard to felting different yarn weights and embellishing techniques.

The knitting techniques are very basic and the felting process can easily be done in your washing machine. So if you think your knitting skills need some help, ask someone to show you how. It's a great way to share some time with family and friends. What better way to celebrate this time of year with a special gift or decoration that you have made yourself.

Sharing from others has helped to make this book possible - so many thanks to Leila Albala, Tina Forrester, Cindy Itovitch, and always, to my Bill.

I wish you happy Christmas seasons for years to come.

Maddy Cranley
August, 1997

About This Book

This book is divided into four parts.

PART ONE. **Basics: Knitting** reviews basic handknitting skills required to complete the felting projects in this book, with emphasis on choosing a suitable yarn and the importance of obtaining correct gauge.

PART TWO. **Basics: Felting** outlines the materials required, methods of felting, how to accurately measure shrinkage, how to apply that information to your pattern measurements, embellishment techniques as well as tips on equipment, supplies and aftercare for your felted projects.

PART THREE. **A Home For The Holidays** contains complete handknitting and felting instructions for home decor items, including several designs of Christmas stockings, a tree skirt and a holiday door hanging.

PART FOUR. **Heartfelt Presents** outlines project directions and patterns for gift giving ideas such as a teddy bear, felted bags, bookmarks and other stocking stuffers.

Finally, at the end you will find a **Mail Order Shopping Guide** and an **Index**.

A Felting Workbook

In PART ONE, you will find a **Workbook Page** that has been designed to guide you in accurately measuring your felting projects. This page encourages you to keep a precise record of changes and shrinkage during the felting process. By keeping an accurate account of your knitting and felting methods for a particular yarn, you will be able to refer to these measurements to repeat a particular process to ensure reliable and consistent results. You will find additional pages of the **Workbook Page** at the end of the book.

At the beginning of a project, you must be disciplined with your knitting and felting methods in order to achieve accuracy. After your "fabric" has been created, you can let your imagination explore all the possibilities of finishing and embellishing techniques.

PART ONE
Basics: Knitting

knitting knitting kni
knitting knitting kni
nitting knitting knitti
tting knitting knitti
g knitting knitting k
ring knitting knitting
nitting knitting knitti
ng knitting knitting
ing knitting knitting
tting knitting knitti
nitting knitting knitti
knitting knitting kn

What You Need To Know

The knowledge of knitting skills required to complete the projects in this book is minimal. Complicated and intricate knitting is not required. The emphasis will be on the felting process and how it can enhance your handknitting to give you an entirely different view of those plain knit and purl stitches. If you can cast on, knit and purl, do simple increases and decreases, and cast off - you've got all you need to complete the projects that are to be found in this book. Some projects will give more seasoned knitters the option of knitting a simple lace pattern edging or an easy two-color plaid pattern.

First, let's review some basic guidelines about choosing yarns, obtaining correct gauge and other fundamental handknitting techniques. There are some details that need particular attention when knitting yarn that will undergo the felting process.

Yarn

In order to ensure that proper felting takes place, it is very important to choose the correct yarn. It is necessary that you use yarns that possess the required properties enabling it to give you the best felting results possible. These yarns must be of 100% animal fibers, such as wool, angora, cashmere, alpaca or mohair. Blends of these animal fiber yarns may also be used. Yarns that consist of synthetics or man-made fibers will not felt well.

The projects in this book are all completed using a basic 100% wool yarn. If you wish to experiment with other animal fibers, you must follow the same procedures that are outlined. The yarns that contain those wonderful fibers like angora, cashmere or mohair can be expensive. Remember, the felting process is *not reversible*. Therefore, be very accurate when testing gauge and felting shrinkage procedures. Once the handknitting has been felted, it cannot be returned to its original size and shape. If you are a beginner to the felting process, I recommend that you choose a 100% wool yarn. This will familiarize you with the felting procedures without the risk of investing in expensive luxury fibers. There is another caution about choosing a yarn type suitable for felting. *Do not use any 100% wool yarn that is labeled "superwash"*. A superwash wool is one that can be washed in a washing machine without fear of shrinkage. These yarns have been treated during production to maintain their properties despite any hot water and agitation thrown in their path. Therefore, these yarns will not felt well.

For the projects in this book, as well as for the following example on obtaining correct gauge, there are three yarn weights that will be most commonly used. A lighter textured felted fabric is produced if using a *sport weight* (24 sts to 4"/10cm) yarn. A *worsted weight* (20 sts to 4"/10cm) yarn is of medium weight and produces a good stable fabric. If you choose to felt a *bulky weight* (14 sts to 4"/10cm) yarn, your felted fabric will be of a much heavier texture and thickness. Whichever weight of yarn you choose to felt, the same rules apply. Select a yarn of 100% animal fiber that is not a "superwash", obtain the correct gauge for that particular yarn, test that sample for felting and carefully measure the results.

Gauge

Gauge (also referred to as "tension") is determined by the type of yarn used, the knitting needle size, the stitch pattern, and the individual knitter. Obtaining the correct gauge for the knitting pattern you have selected is always very important. Whatever you do when it comes to knitting a project that will be felted - *do not eliminate knitting a gauge sample!* If you do not obtain the correct gauge in your knitted sample, your mistake will be multiplied when it comes to felting that knitting. Knit those samples, please!

Following, you will find a checklist to use as a guide to obtaining the correct gauge. It is recommended that you knit a large sample, at least 8" (20cm) square. The results obtained on a large sample will more accurately give you measurements that you can apply to larger pieces of knitting or pattern pieces. If you are just testing a particular yarn, ensure that you obtain the gauge as stated on the ball band. If you are testing a yarn for a specific pattern, you must match the required gauge as stated in the knitting pattern instructions.

Once you have obtained the correct knitting gauge, you will use this same sample to test the felting process.

Knitting Your Sample

As it will be possible to use different yarn weights to complete the projects in this book, the following information about gauge is given for three yarn weights - sport, worsted and bulky.

✔ **Select your yarn**
- 100% wool or animal fiber blend (not a "superwash")
  Sport .... approx 164yd (150m) per 1¾oz (50g) ball
  Worsted .... approx 114yd (104m) per 1¾oz (50g) ball
  Bulky .... approx 120yd (110m) per 3½oz (100g) ball

✔ **Read gauge**
- stated on ball band or in knitting pattern instructions
- measured over 4" (10cm) of stocking stitch
  Sport .... 24 sts x 30 rows using 3.75mm (CAN9/US5) needles
  Worsted .... 20 sts x 26 rows using 4.5mm (CAN7/US7) needles
  Bulky .... 14 sts x 20 rows using 6mm (CAN4/US10) needles

✔ **Cast on**
- work in stocking stitch
  Sport .... 48 sts for 60 rows
  Worsted .... 40 sts for 52 rows
  Bulky .... 28 sts for 40 rows

✔ **Measure stitches and rows**
Lay the sample flat. With pins, mark out a 4" (10cm) square on the knitting, making sure you are 1" (2.5cm) from the edges of the sample. Count the number of stitches and rows between the marker pins.
If you have *less* than 24 (20, 14) sts or 30 (26, 20) rows within the marked square, change to a *smaller* needle size.
If you have *more* than 24 (20, 14) sts or 30 (26, 20) rows within the marked square, change to a *larger* needle size.

A good investment is a gauge ruler or gauge square. These accessories will define either a 1" (2.5cm) or 4" (10cm) area and allow for easier counting of the stitches and rows.

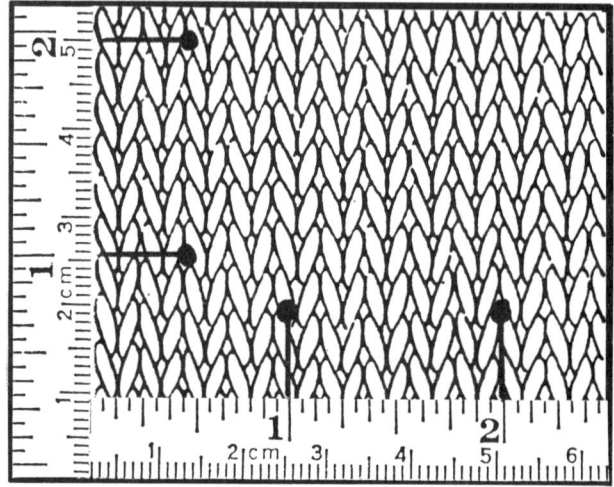

Fig. 1.1 Measuring Gauge on Sample

✔ **Measure Sample**
To double check your gauge, verify that your sample measures 8" (20cm) wide and 8" (20cm) long. If your sample has these measurements, you have obtained a gauge of:

Sport .... 24 sts x 30 rows
Worsted .... 20 sts x 26 rows
Bulky .... 14 sts x 20 rows

If your sample is *wider* or *longer* than 8" (20cm) wide or 8" (20cm) long, change to a *smaller* needle size.

If your sample is *narrower* or *shorter* than 8" (20cm) wide or 8" (20cm) long, change to a *larger* needle size.

Knitting Needle Conversion Chart

Metric	Canadian/UK	US
2mm	14	0
2.25mm	13	1
2.75mm	12	2
3mm	11	3
3.25mm	10	4
3.75mm	9	5
4mm	8	6
4.5mm	7	7
5mm	6	8
5.5mm	5	9
6mm	4	10
6.5mm	3	-
7mm	2	10½
7.5mm	1	11
8mm	0	13
9mm	00	15

Casting On

Placing that first row of stitches onto your needle is always important. For handknitting that will be felted, a stable rather than an elastic edge is needed. The following method for casting on, called a Cable or Knitted Cast On, will produce a neat edge that has evenly spaced stitches that are neither too tight nor too loose on the needle.

Cable or Knitted Cast On

1. Make a slip knot and place the loop on the left-hand needle.
2. Insert the right-hand needle into the loop from front to back and bringing the yarn over the point of the right-hand needle from the back, draw the yarn through the slip knot loop to make a stitch.
3. Place the stitch made onto the left-hand needle and continue to make the required number of stitches by inserting the right-hand needle *between* the last two stitches worked.

Binding Off

Just as it is important to get those stitches onto the needles in a correct fashion, we must also take them off the needles to create a secure edge that will not unravel or lose its shape.

The following method of binding off works best on a knit row. If used on a purl row, all stitches should be worked purlwise.

1. Knit the first two stitches.
2. Insert the tip of the left-hand needle through the first stitch on the right-hand needle and lift it over the second stitch, allowing it to fall off the needle.
3. Knit the next stitch and lift the first stitch on the right-hand hand needle over the second stitch, being careful not to knit the stitches too tightly as this may distort your edge.
4. Work as in Step 3 until one stitch remains. Cut the yarn and slip the end through the remaining stitch. Pull the yarn to tighten and fasten off.

Increasing/Decreasing

For the knitting projects in this book, the simple method of increasing and decreasing is used. On certain edges, the increases or decreases are worked on the second stitch of the row and on the second to last stitch of the row. This increases the stability of the edge of the knitted piece. The individual pattern instructions will indicate whether this variation of the method is to be used.

Increasing
1. Knit into the front of the stitch to make one stitch. Do not slip the old stitch off the left-hand needle.
2. Knit into the back of the same stitch to make another stitch.
3. Slip the old stitch off the left-hand needle. You now have two stitches transferred to the right-hand needle.

Decreasing
1. On a knit row, knit two stitches together.
2. On a purl row, purl two stitches together.

Duplicate Stitch (Swiss Darning)

Duplicate stitch is an embroidery stitch that is worked on stocking (stockinette) stitch to cover or duplicate an original knitted stitch, either to add a color or even correct a mistake by working the correct color over a wrong one. For the felting projects in this book, duplicate stitch will be worked on the knitted piece *before* felting. This will ensure that the duplicate stitch will take on the same shrinkage percentage as the knitted piece. Be sure to match the yarn weight used for the duplicate stitch to that used for the background knitting.

Fig. 1.2 Horizontal Duplicate Stitch

Fig. 1.3 Vertical Duplicate Stitch

Horizontal Duplicate Stitch (Fig. 1.2)
1. Bring the needle out to the right side of knitting at the base of the stitch to be covered.
2. Insert the needle under the two strands of the stitch above, pull the yarn through and insert needle at same point of entry.
3. Continue to work on the knitting from right to left.

Vertical Duplicate Stitch (Fig. 1.3)
1. Bring the needle out to the right side of knitting at the base of the stitch to be covered.
2. Insert the needle under the two strands of the stitch above, pull the yarn through and insert needle at same point of entry, bringing needle out to the right side at base of the next stitch to be covered.
3. Continue to work on the knitting from bottom to top.

The Workbook Page

The Workbook Page (shown opposite) acts as an aid in keeping accurate measurements of your knitting gauge and felting technique. In the future, you will be able to refer to this written record of the performance of a particular yarn and therefore guarantee consistent results. Additional copies of the Workbook Page can be found at the end of the book.

Make note of the yarn brand name, the color name, number and the dye lot. Knit your sample, entering the number of stitches cast on, the number of rows knit and the needle size used.

Enter the gauge you have obtained on the line "Gauge (before felting)". If you are testing the gauge for a particular project, ensure that the gauge of the knitted sample matches the gauge required in the pattern instructions. Record the width and length measurements of the knitted sample on the diagram titled "Before Felting". The balance of the Workbook Page will be completed as you test your knitted sample through the felting process in PART TWO.

Machine Knitting

The knitting patterns and project instructions in this book are written for the handknitter. Practical considerations, though, do not allow for the complete disregard of the efficiency and speed afforded by the knitting machine.

Some of the felting projects featured in PART THREE and PART FOUR require a handknitted square or rectangle of stocking (stockinette) stitch. These sections could easily be completed on a very basic knitting machine or knitting frame. The measurements given for the handknitted pieces as well as the after felting measurements would apply to any knitting produced on a knitting machine. If speed is a priority to you, a knitting machine can certainly complete your projects in much quicker time.

If you do choose to machine-knit any of the projects, remember that the basic rules apply - choose your yarn carefully, obtain the correct gauge for the yarn and record your felting process accurately.

Workbook Page

Yarn: _____   Color name: _____

Color No: _____   Dye lot: _____

Sample knit: _____ sts x _____ rows   Needle size: _____

Gauge (before felting): _____ sts x _____ rows to 4" (10cm)

<u>KNITTED SAMPLE MEASUREMENTS</u>

" (cm) width   " (cm) width

" (cm)   "(cm)
length   length

Before Felting   After Felting

Felting method used: _____

Time: _____

Gauge (after felting): _____ sts x _____ rows to 4" (10cm)

Percentage of shrinkage:
(Before Felting Gauge x 100 ÷ After Felting Gauge = Percentage of Shrinkage)

Stitch Gauge: _____ x 100 ÷ _____ = _____ %

Row Gauge: _____ x 100 ÷ _____ = _____ %

Knitting Abbreviations

alt	alternate
approx	approximately
beg	begin(ning)
circ	circular
CC	contrast color
cont	continu(e)(ing)
dec	decreas(e)(ing)
foll	follow(s)(ing)
inc	increas(e)(ing)
K(k)	knit
kwise	knitwise
LH	left-hand
MC	main color
P(p)	purl
patt(s)	pattern(s)
psso	pass slipped stitch(es) over
pwise	purlwise
RH	right-hand
RS	right side(s) of work
rem	remain(s)(ing)
rep	repeat(ing)
rev st st	reverse stocking (stockinette) stitch
sc	single crochet
sl	slip
st(s)	stitch(es)
st st	stocking (stockinette) stitch
tbl	through back loop(s)
tog	together
WS	wrong side(s) of work
wyib	with yarn in back of work
wyif	with yarn in front of work
yo	yarn over needle
*	repeat directions following * as many times as indicated

PART TWO
Basics: Felting

felting felting felting
felting felting felting
felting felting felting
felting felting felting
felting felting felting
felting felting felting
felting felting felting
felting felting felting
felting felting felting
felting felting felting
felting felting felting
felting felting felting
felting felting felting

Felting, Fulling Or Boiled Wool?
A Definition

The terms "felting", "fulling" and "boiled wool" all describe a process, which takes an animal fiber yarn and by application of heat, moisture and mechanical action or agitation causes an interlocking or matting of the yarn fibers to create a dense fabric. The most suitable fiber with good felting properties is wool but other animal fibers such as mohair, angora, alpaca or cashmere can be felted. What makes these fibers suitable for felting is their surface structure of overlapping scales, which possess a high degree of crimp or waviness. When placed in hot water and rubbed together, these scales mix and glide over each other intertwining to create that dense fabric we call felt. Carded wool in batts is also used to create felt. In this book, all felting will have its beginnings in handknitted yarn.

The origin of the word "felt" likely had its start in the word "filz" from Old High German. One of the earliest handknitted garments recorded is the Monmouth Cap, a felted knit hat that was first produced in the 13th century in Coventry, England.

The word "fulling" stems from "fullare", a Medieval Latin word meaning "to walk on or trample". Fuller's Earth, more often seen on a pharmacy or health food store shelf, is a highly adsorptive material consisting of a variety of clay and minerals. Known for its drying qualities and pulling power, it was so named as it was used by textile workers or "fullers" to remove grease and oils from cloth. Today, we are more likely to see it used as an ingredient in a face mask, where it sets its pulling power to other tasks.

"Boiled wool" is another descriptive term for felted cloth. It is the characteristic fabric used to fashion those chic Tyrolean jackets embellished with matching braid binding and pewter buttons. The basic process is the same as for "felting" or "fulling", taking 100% wool yarn through the stages of dyeing, knitting and shrinking in hot water without the aid of chemicals. Again, the result is a dense, warm and windproof fabric that still remains lightweight with a soft hand. From this point on, in regard to this process, it will be referred to as "felting". So let's take a closer look and see how you can start to felt your handknitting.

Felting Your Knitted Sample

You have chosen a yarn suitable for felting and attained the correct gauge for that yarn, as stated on the ball band or as required in the knitting pattern instructions. The next step is to test the knitted sample through the felting process. You will then be able to determine what percentage of shrinkage this particular yarn will undergo. On a Workbook Page, you will have noted the gauge of the knitted sample as well as the width and the length of the sample.

Following is a list of the basic materials you will need to begin the felting process. The next step is to choose a felting method, either by hand or in the washing machine, and complete the procedure as outlined.

What You Need

✔ **Knitted Sample**
 - a large sample, at least 8" (20cm) square
 - knit in a yarn suitable for felting
 - knit to the correct gauge according to the ball band or the knitting pattern instructions

✔ **Pure Soap Flakes**
 - not ordinary laundry <u>detergent</u>
 - the product label should state *pure soap* (readily available in natural product stores)

✔ **Baking Soda**
 - to aid in creating a sudsy solution

✔ **Towel**
 - for drying, if felting by hand
 - for agitation, if felting in the washing machine

✔ **Rubber Gloves**
 - if felting by hand

✔ **Timer**

Felting Methods

Now that you have gathered the basic materials to felt your knitted sample by hand or in the washing machine, ensure that you will be using the same method for testing your sample that will be used for felting the completed knitting project.

Felting by hand requires more muscle power than felting in the washing machine, but it has its satisfactions. It is somewhat akin to baking bread. If you have the prescribed temperament, felting cloth or kneading dough can become one of those therapeutic activities that bonds us with all those who have ever undertaken these ancient crafts. Felting by hand is suitable for small projects but becomes a bit more cumbersome when you are felting larger pieces or complete garments. Felting by hand does afford the opportunity to be more accurate by allowing for more frequent taking of measurements during the felting process.

Whichever felting method you choose, it is most important to remember that you record accurately all the measurements and changes. You will then be able to either adjust or repeat the method to produce reliable and consistent results.

Yarns with the same brand name but of a different color, may felt differently. Again, always test a sample. You may also find that some yarns have to undergo the felting method more than once in order to achieve the desired result. Be sure to record any additional felting procedures.

As these yarns will be going into very hot water, colorfastness can be affected. Again, testing a sample will give you an indication of how different colors will react. If you are planning to felt a project that will be knit in two or more colors, it is always advisable to test those same colors together on a knitted sample.

Any knitting that has properly felted, no matter what method has been used, will have a distinct texture. The knitted piece becomes very dense and matted. This will be one of the key criteria for determining that felting has occurred. If you hold the felted sample up to a strong light, you will not be able to clearly distinguish the grid of stitches and rows. This textural appearance and the measurement changes confirm that felting has taken place.

By Hand

Depending on the size of the piece to be felted, use a large sink or bowl filled with water as hot as you can tolerate while wearing rubber gloves. Measure the sample often to monitor felting.

✔ Soak the knitted sample or project for ½ hour in the hot water.

✔ Add the soap flakes and the baking soda in a 4 to 1 ratio, never using less than ¼ cup (60ml) of soap flakes. Agitate the piece(s) by kneading and rubbing, until felting has taken place. Verify this by taking measurements and carefully observing the textural appearance.

✔ If more felting is necessary, repeat the previous two steps.

✔ Rinse the felted piece(s) in cool water. Gently squeeze out the excess water.

✔ Roll the felted piece(s) in a towel and let rest for 15 minutes.

✔ On a flat surface, shape the felted piece(s) by squaring up the edges or pinning to the desired measurements of the knitting pattern instructions. Allow to dry thoroughly before cutting or embellishing.

✔ If an edge flares, baste a thread through the edge and gather in. Remove the thread after the felting is dry.

✔ When dry, brush the felting for a softer surface.

By Washing Machine

✔ Place the knitted sample or project in the washing machine with a large towel (in a non-interfering color) for agitation.

✔ Set the washing machine to a low water setting if felting a sample or small knitted piece. Set to a higher water setting for larger or multiple pieces.

✔ Set the water temperature to the hottest setting (usually "Hot" or "Whites") and to the longest cycle.

✔ Add ½ cup (125ml) of soap flakes and 2 tablespoons (30ml) of baking soda for a small load. Add 1 cup (250ml) of soap flakes and 4 tablespoons (60ml) of baking soda for larger or multiple pieces of knitting.

✔ Run through a normal washing cycle, removing every five minutes to verify for desired shrinkage and felted textural appearance.

✔ If more felting is required, repeat the previous five steps.

✔ Run through the rinse and spin dry cycle.

✔ On a flat surface, shape the felted piece(s) by squaring up the edges or pinning to the desired measurements of the knitting pattern instructions. Allow to dry thoroughly before cutting or embellishing.

✔ If an edge flares, baste a thread through the edge and gather in. Remove the thread after the felting is dry.

✔ When dry, brush the felting for a softer surface.

Shrinkage Percentages

Enter the felted measurements of both width and length of the sample on the diagram titled "After Felting" on a Workbook Page.

To determine the after felting gauge, divide the number of stitches cast on for the knitted sample by the width of the felted sample (e.g., 40 sts ÷ 7"/18cm = 22.5 sts to 4"/10cm) and divide the number of rows knit for the knitted sample by the length of the felted sample, (e.g., 52 rows ÷ 6¼"/16cm = 33 rows to 4"/10cm). Enter the results of these calculations on the "Gauge (after felting)" line on a Workbook Page. (Note: Calculations may vary slightly between the imperial and metric measurements.)

Now that you have determined the gauge of the felted sample, you will be able to calculate the shrinkage percentages that occurred during felting by applying this simple formula:

Gauge Before Felting × 100% = Percentage of Shrinkage
Gauge After Felting

Example:
Stitch Gauge: Row Gauge:
20 × 100 = 88%   26 × 100 = 79%
22.5   33

After felting, the sample is 88% of the width and 79% of the length of the knitted sample *before* felting.

These are the percentages of shrinkage that have occurred during the felting of the knitted sample. These will be the percentages you will use to determine how much that particular type of yarn will felt when you are using it to knit a specific knitting pattern.

If certain or required shrinkage percentages have not been attained or the knitted sample does not have the desired textural felted appearance, repeat the felting method.

The pattern and project instructions that are to follow in PART THREE and PART FOUR of this book will state a required shrinkage percentage. The shrinkage percentage may vary a small amount, but to be accurate, should not vary more than one or two per cent.

If you choose to knit and felt other patterns, you can, with a few more calculations, determine what size to knit. You will take the shrinkage percentages of the felted sample, that has been knit in a particular yarn, and apply them to the knitting pattern that you wish to complete using that same yarn. What is most important to remember is that one calculation of percentage of shrinkage applies to the width and stitches measurements and the other calculation of percentage applies to the length and rows measurements.

Example:
1. A knitting pattern states a required gauge of 26 sts × 32 rows = 4" (10cm) over st st.
2. You have chosen a yarn with felting properties, obtained the correct knitting gauge and tested a sample for felting shrinkage. After felting, the gauge is 28 sts × 36.5 rows = 4" (10cm) over st st.

3. Determine the shrinkage percentages:

Stitch Gauge:

$$\frac{26}{28} \times 100 = 92\%$$

Row Gauge:

$$\frac{32}{36.5} \times 100 = 87\%$$

4. For the pattern you have chosen, all stitch measurements (width) will shrink to 92% of stated size. All row measurements (length) will shrink to 87% of stated size.

5. For any stitch or width measurement instruction in the knitting pattern, divide that number by .92 to determine what instruction you must knit in order to obtain the correct size *after* felting.

Example:

Desired finished bust size: 40" (102cm)

Apply the width shrinkage percentage:

40" (102cm) ÷ .92 = 43" (109cm)

Knit the pattern instruction for the finished bust size closest to 43" (109cm).

6. For any row or length measurement instruction in the knitting pattern, divide that number by .87 to determine what instruction you must knit in order to obtain the correct size *after* felting.

Example:

Pattern Instruction: "Work even for 10" (25cm)."

Apply the length shrinkage percentage:

10" (25cm) ÷ .87 = 11½" (29cm)

Knit the pattern instruction as: "Work even for 11½" (29cm)."

A Review

These are the basic guidelines that should be applied to any handknitting that you may wish to felt.

✔   Choose a yarn that has felting properties.

✔   Knit a large sample to the correct gauge, as stated on the ball band or in the knitting pattern instructions.

✔   Measure the knitted sample before felting.

✔   Felt the knitted sample by hand or washing machine.

✔ Measure the felted sample.

✔ Calculate the shrinkage percentages of stitches and rows.

✔ Verify that these are the required shrinkage percentages in the knitting pattern instructions.

How To Enlarge Patterns

In PART THREE and PART FOUR, you will find projects that require you to cut a pattern piece from a section of felting. These pattern pieces are laid out on a graph with a ¼" grid and will have to be enlarged four times to obtain a full-size pattern. There are two ways that you can make these enlargements.

1. **Photocopying**
   Using the "enlarge" button on the photocopier, increase the size of the pattern (usually 400%) until the graph is shown to have a 1" (2.5cm) square grid.

2. **Grid Method**
   Copy the pattern, one square at a time, onto graph paper that has a 1" (2.5cm) square grid.

The Cutting Edge

You will find that some of the projects require the felted knitting to be cut out in pattern pieces and remain without further finishing to the edges. It is important that these pieces of felting are cut carefully, using sharp scissors or blades, to eliminate any ragged edges.

A rotary blade is an excellent tool if cutting a long continuous line or larger pattern pieces of the felting. This tool also affords the option of using decorative blades, which can create "pinked" or "wave" finished edges.

Pointed trimmers and small embroidery scissors are very helpful in cutting out detailed pieces or for reaching into awkward areas.

Save any remnants of felting that result from your cutting as these can be later put to use as decorative pieces to applique or piece together to create a patchwork effect.

Seams

For all projects in this book, you will be joining *felted* pieces of knitting. As the felted knitting is somewhat bulkier than regular knitting, use a flat seam to join sections of felting. This will create a seam that, when opened out, will lie flat.

Join all seams using a No. 14 "sharp" yarn needle to facilitate sewing through the felted fabric. Join the seams using matching yarn, sewing thread, or invisible nylon thread. Using the sewing or invisible thread creates a more invisible seam but be careful that it is not used on seams that will undergo a lot of stress. Sewing and invisible thread arc suitable for joining pieces of felting if the seams are to be overcast with yarn and embroidery stitching such as the blanket, cross, whip or herringbone stitch. (See An Embroidery Primer, page 32). These embroidery stitches, as well as being decorative, will further strengthen the seam. When joining sections of a felted project, it is always best to work each seam in the same direction, (e.g., top to bottom, left side to right side) in order to maintain the same tension in the finished or completed project.

To join the seam, hold the two pieces of felted fabric to be joined with the right sides together. The needle is drawn through the very edge stitch on the front piece and then through the very edge stitch on the back piece. The yarn (or thread) is pulled through in an overcast stitch action and repeated, with the needle being placed through exactly the same part of each edge every time. If you do not follow along the edge as closely as possible the seam will never lie flat. Check periodically to ensure that the stitches are close together and are secure enough to close the seam but not too tight so as to create puckering.

In some of the projects, you will be required to cut out a section of felting and inset this section into another piece of felting that has a matching cut-out area. Place the inset piece into the cut-out area, matching the edges and keeping work flat. On the wrong side of work, with an overcast stitch action, join edges of the cut-out to the main piece of felting. After joining, turn work to the right side and with a steam iron and a damp cloth, *lightly* press the seam.

An Embroidery Primer

Once your felted knitting has become more like a "fabric", it will lend itself very well as a background for embroidery stitches. The embroidery can be completed using yarn or embroidery thread and a No. 14 "sharp" yarn needle.

The blanket stitch (Fig. 2.1) and the whip stitch (Fig. 2.2) are very effective stitches to finish the edges of your felting. They can also be used to create decorative border effects.

The back stitch (Fig. 2.3) and the cross stitch (Fig 2.4) are attractive stitches to join seams and attach cut-out pieces of felting to a background.

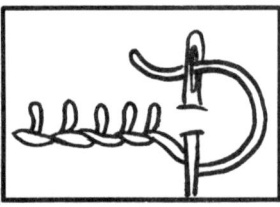

Fig. 2.1 Blanket Stitch
Bring needle up on right side, hold thread under left thumb, insert needle about ¼" (7mm) to the right and bring it out through loop held by left thumb.

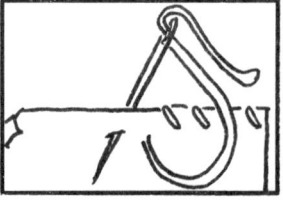

Fig. 2.2 Whip Stitch
Working from right to left, make slanted stitches about ¼" (7mm) apart, encasing edge of fabric.

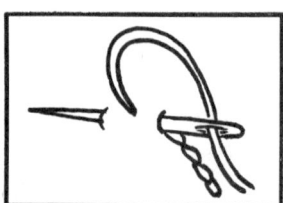

Fig. 2.3 Back Stitch
Working from right to left, bring needle up on right side. Take a stitch backward, bring the needle up an equal distance ahead of the first hole made by the thread. Repeat, taking the needle back to the beginning of the previous stitch.

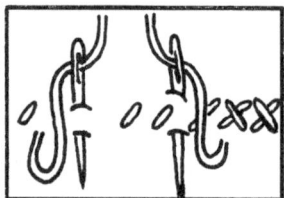

Fig. 2.4 Cross Stitch
Working from left to right, make a row of even diagonal stitches. Work back again, with the top half pointing from bottom to top left.

Making A Twisted Cord

A decorative twisted cord with a tassel finish can add a practical and decorative touch to a felted project. Using different colors and textures of yarn as well as varying the number of strands can add to its versatility. The cord will vary in thickness according to the number of strands you choose. Four strands will result in a twisted cord with a thickness of eight strands.

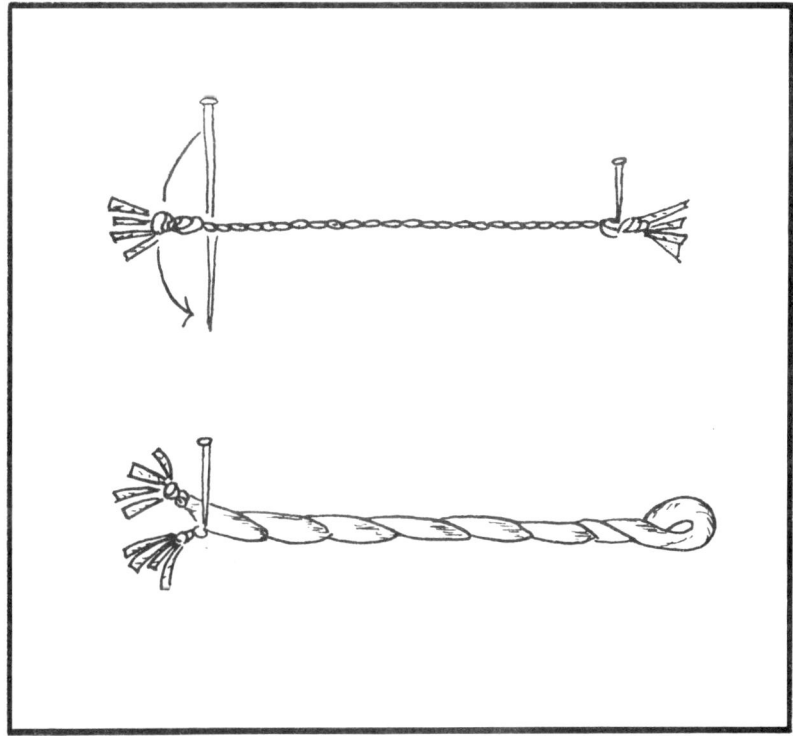

Fig. 2.5 Making A Twisted Cord

Twisted Cord

1. To determine what length the strands of yarn need to be, multiply the desired *finished* length of cord by 3 (e.g., 36" /92cm to result in a 12"/30.5cm cord).
2. Cut the strands of yarn, making sure all ends are even.

3. Knot all the strands together about 1" (2.5cm) from each end.
4. Insert a small knitting needle through each knot or if working alone secure one end to a hook or door handle. Twist the knitting needle(s) counterclockwise until the strands are tightly twisted and the cord begins to twist back on itself.
5. Holding at the center of the cord, and keeping the cord taut, bring the two ends together and knot above original knots. Remove the knitting needle(s) or release from hook or door handle.
6. Release the center of the cord and allow it to twist together, smoothing it down from the knotted ends to folded end.
7. Knot the cord at folded end. Cut the folded end, leaving enough length to form a tassel.
8. Undo the original knots from opposite end and cut strands into an even length to form a tassel.

Making A Knitted Cord

This knitted cord can find many applications such as a decorative edging, a loop for a Christmas stocking or a ribbon-like closure to tie in a bow. The following knitting instructions will produce a knitted tube of stocking (stockinette) stitch. This tubular cord, if *lightly* pressed will lie flat, taking on the appearance of decorative braid, which can be used to finish cut edges of felting.

Knitted Cord
1. Use double-pointed needles in the size that will give you the correct gauge for the yarn weight you have chosen. (See Knitting Your Sample, page 13)
2. Cast on ...
   Sport .... 6 sts
   Worsted .... 5 sts
   Bulky .... 4 sts
3. *Knit all sts. Do not turn work but slide stitches to the end of the needle. Repeat from * until desired length is obtained. (Note: Always knit first stitch of the row firmly, to maintain a smooth cord with an even tension.)

Beyond The Fringe

Adding a fringe, by knotting strands of yarn to the edges of felting, can add yet another ornamental finish. You can choose a yarn weight for the fringe that matches the yarn weight used to complete the project, or you may wish to select a yarn or fiber in a contrast color or complementary texture to add a hint of your own creativity.

Attached Fringe

1. To determine what length the strands of yarn need to be, double the desired *finished* length of the fringe and add 1" (2.5cm) for knotting, (e.g., 5"/12.5cm strands to result in a 2"/5cm fringe).

2. Cut a piece of light cardboard into a square with sides equal to the measurement of the strand. Fold the cardboard in half and wrap yarn around the fold. Cut the strands free from the cardboard at the open end.

3. Take the number of strands required and fold in half. With a crochet hook, draw the loop through the edge of the felting. Draw the loose ends of the strands through the loop and pull down to form a knot (Fig. 2.6).

4. After the fringe is attached on the edge of the felting, trim to an even length.

Fig. 2.6 Attaching Fringe

Tassels

A tassel, unlike a fringe, can stand on its own. It can be a singular compliment to a completed task. If you think of a tassel as a decorative punctuation, you will take the chance and experiment by working the tassel in a variety of fibers and colors to enhance your project and say "it's done!"

Basic Tassel

1. Wrap yarn around a 3" (8cm) square of cardboard, 30 or 40 times or until there are enough strands for a plump tassel.
2. With a separate length of yarn, tie the strands together tightly at one edge of the cardboard (Fig. 2.7).
3. Cut the other end of strands free from the cardboard. With a separate length of yarn, at a point 1" (2.5cm) down from tie, wrap the entire bundle and secure ends (Fig. 2.8).

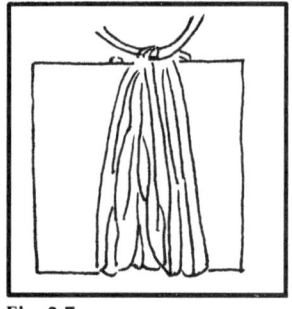
Fig. 2.7

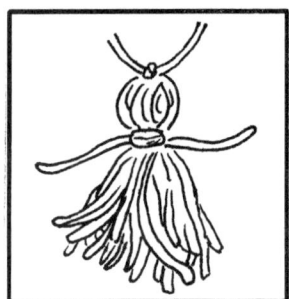
Fig. 2.8

Aftercare

After you have completed your handknitting and placed it through the felting process, you may think that it has gone through the most vigorous and tortured wash that knitted yarn could ever endure. Now and forever more, you assume that you can throw that felted project into the hot wash cycle along with your sheets. Don't do it! I caution you to treat your newly felted projects carefully in order to avoid further distortion or shrinkage.

You have spent a lot of time and care completing these items through the knitting and felting stages. A little thought to its aftercare will ensure that you will have these beautiful felted pieces for many years to come.

✔ Hand wash the felting, using a mild soap or special wool detergent and lukewarm water.

✔ Squeeze the suds into the felting. Do not rub as further felting may occur. Do not leave felting to soak.

✔ Rinse twice with lukewarm water, adding fabric softener to last rinse, if so desired.

✔ Roll felting into a towel and squeeze out as much excess water as possible.

✔ Lay felting onto a dry towel, away from direct heat or sunlight.

✔ Shape felting to correct measurements.

✔ Allow to dry thoroughly. Do not use a clothes dryer.

✔ If storing for a length of time, be sure to include a moth repellent tucked inside the woolen items.

Felted handknitting can always be improved with brushing. Even a slight pressing will give a smoother appearance to the felted fabric. Always press *lightly* using a steam iron and a damp cloth. Never press down on the fabric but hold the iron just above the fabric.

PART THREE

A Home For The Holidays

the holidays a home
days a home for the
home for the holiday
e holidays a home f
s a home for the ho
for the holidays a h
lidays a home for t
home for the holiday
the holidays a home
lays a home for the
me for the holidays
e holidays a home fo
s a home for the hol

ABOVE, LEFT TO RIGHT:
Felted Christmas stockings, "Fringe and Tinsel" (D), "Eyelet and Ribbons" (E), "Lattice and Beads" (B), "Ribbons and Stars" (A), "Stars and Lace" (C).
BELOW LEFT: *Felted Christmas hanging.*
BELOW RIGHT: *Felted Christmas tree skirt.*

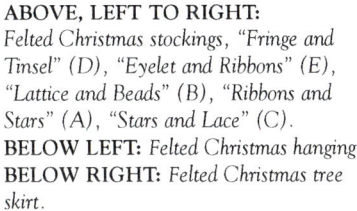

A Home For The Holidays

When we set out to decorate our homes for the holiday season, the intention is to dress up our surroundings to give them some seasonal charm. We want to make our everyday environment look different and special for this time of year. Yet, we tend to revert to the same age-old traditions in order to maintain a strong continuity in our annual celebrations.

The Christmas color palette is one tradition that remains very constant in our decorating plans. Red and green are the typical colors displayed for this holiday season, but we can take this conventional color palette and vary it by choosing from the many hues and shades of these two colors.

In this section of the book, you will find three different projects to dress up your home for the holidays. There are Christmas stockings styled with beads, ribbons and decorative cut edges, a tree skirt adorned with a stencil-look angel motif to accent your holiday pine or spruce, and a winter scene hanging that can make an appearance long before the special day and remain on your door or over your fireplace into the long winter days of January.

Christmas Stockings

Christmas stockings are a very traditional decoration customarily found in the familiar setting hung on a fireplace mantle. They can be both decorative and of course functional, if you wish to fill them with small gifts and tokens.

Try hanging a stocking in a different place such as your front door or in a frosty window. Complete the stockings with a different color on each side and this will give you a change of decor during the Christmas season. Don't forget to mix and match all those wonderful hues of reds and greens to result in an eclectic look to your stocking collection. Choose a variety of yarn weights in which to complete the stockings - a bulky weight for a more rustic look, worsted weight for a medium texture or a sport weight for a finer finish. The instructions that are to follow will result in one size of stocking, the variety abounds in color choice, yarn weight and how you choose to embellish your stocking.

The Basic Christmas Stocking

FINISHED SIZE

The finished size for all styles of Christmas stockings is the measurement after felting the knitting and assembly of the stocking.
Finished length of stocking (from top edge to base of heel)
17" (43cm)
Finished size of cuff (width x depth)
(15 x 6)" or (38 x 15)cm

MATERIALS

The yarn amounts listed in the Basic Stocking Chart and the Basic Cuff Chart (see pages 45 and 46), are what you will need, in a selected yarn weight of a 100% animal fiber, to complete two sides of one stocking and one cuff. Any additional yarn and materials requirements are listed for each style of stocking in quantities sufficient to embellish both sides of the stocking.

GAUGE

Knit a large sample, in the yarn weight you have chosen, at least 8" (20cm) square, to test both knitting gauge and felting shrinkage, as listed in the Basic Stocking and the Basic Cuff Charts.
(See Knitting Your Sample, page 13 and Felting Your Knitted Sample, page 24)

SHRINKAGE PERCENTAGES

$\dfrac{\text{Gauge Before Felting}}{\text{Gauge After Felting}}$ x 100% = Percentage of Shrinkage

Example (using worsted weight yarn):

Stitch Gauge: Row Gauge:

$\dfrac{20}{22.5}$ x 100 = 88% $\dfrac{26}{33}$ x 100 = 79%

These are the percentages of shrinkage that must occur during the felting of the knitted sample in order to obtain the correct finished size.
The felted sample should be 88% of the width and 79% of the length of the knitted sample *before* felting.

INSTRUCTIONS

1. Follow the Basic Stocking Chart (see below), and knit *two* stocking sections, *reversing* shaping for second section.
2. Follow the Basic Cuff Chart (see page 46), and knit one cuff.
3. Felt the knitted pieces to obtain felted measurements as listed.

(continued on page 47)

Basic Stocking Chart

Yarn Weight	*Sport*	*Worsted*	*Bulky*
No. of Balls (MC)	5 (1¾oz/50g) each approx (164yd/150m)	5 (1¾oz/50g) each approx (114yd/104m)	3 (3½oz/100g) each approx (120yd/110m)
Needle Size (suggested)	3.75mm (CAN9/US5)	4.5mm (CAN7/US7)	6mm (CAN4/US10)
Knitting Gauge (4"/10cm over st st)	24 sts x 30 rows	20 sts x 26 rows	14 sts x 20 rows
Shrinkage %: (approximate) *WIDTH* *LENGTH*	80% 70%	88% 79%	86% 82%
Cast on ...	115 sts	86 sts	62 sts
Work in st st ...	70 rows	52 rows	40 rows
Bind off at beg of next row ...	38 sts	30 sts	21 sts
Cont in st st ...	146 rows	112 rows	82 rows
Bind off ...	77 sts	56 sts	41 sts
Felted Size (Fig. 3.1, page 46) *A* *B* *C* *D*	10" (25cm) 19½" (50cm) 15" (38cm) 6¼" (16cm)	10" (25cm) 19½" (50cm) 15" (38cm) 6¼" (16cm)	10" (25cm) 19½" (50cm) 15" (38cm) 6¼" (16cm)

Fig. 3.1 Felted Measurement Guide for Basic Stocking and Cuff

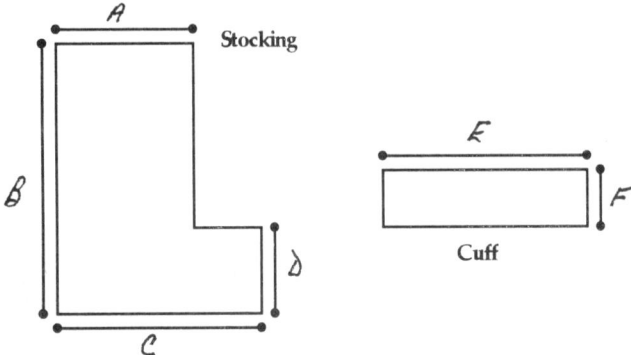

Basic Cuff Chart

Yarn Weight	*Sport*	*Worsted*	*Bulky*
No. of Balls (CC)	1 (1¾oz/50g) each approx (164yd/150m)	1 (1¾oz/50g) each approx (114yd/104m)	2 (3½oz/100g) each approx (120yd/110m)
Needle Size (suggested)	3.75mm (CAN9/US5)	4.5mm (CAN7/US7)	6mm (CAN4/US10)
Knitting Gauge (4"/10cm over st st)	24 sts x 30 rows	20 sts x 26 rows	14 sts x 20 rows
Shrinkage %: (approximate) WIDTH LENGTH	80% 70%	88% 79%	86% 82%
Cast on ...	114 sts	86 sts	62 sts
Work in st st ...	66 rows	50 rows	38 rows
Bind off ...	114 sts	86 sts	62 sts
Felted Size (Fig. 3.1) WIDTH (E) DEPTH (F)	15" (38cm) 6" (15cm)	15" (38cm) 6" (15cm)	15" (38cm) 6" (15cm)

(continued from page 45)

4. Enlarge the Basic Stocking Pattern (Fig. 3.2) until grid squares measure 1" (2.5cm). From one felted piece (RS up), cut one stocking side. *Reverse* the stocking pattern (RS down) on RS of other felted piece and cut second stocking side.
5. Refer to the instructions for each style to complete the stocking.

Fig. 3.2 Basic Stocking Pattern

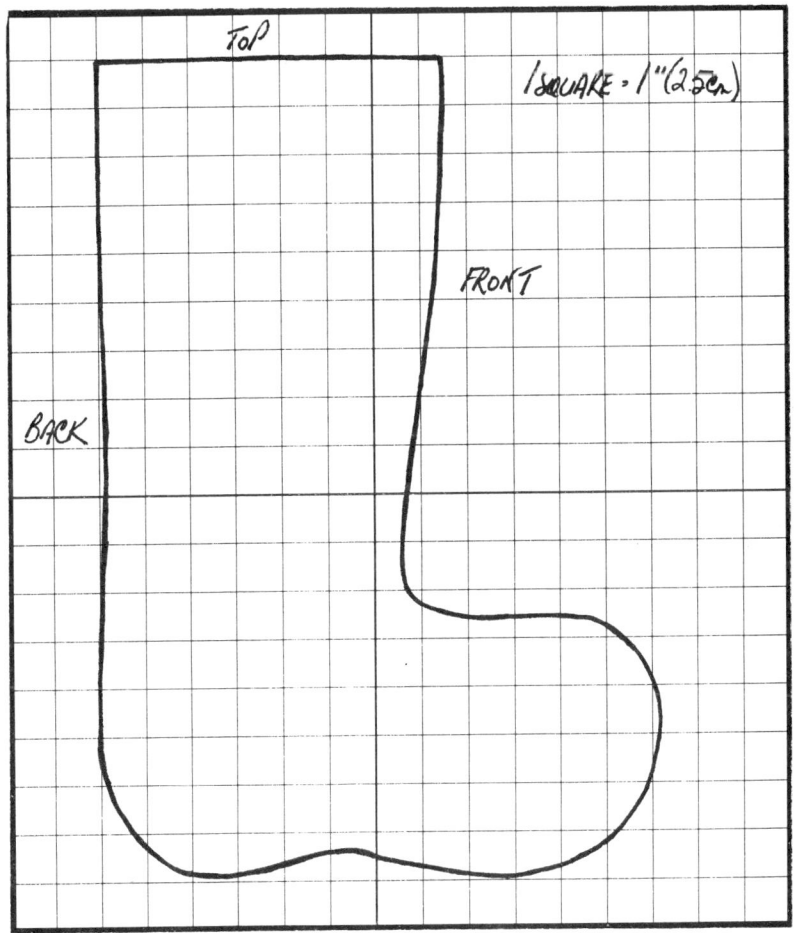

Style A - Ribbons and Stars (See cover and page 41)
MATERIALS
1 Basic Stocking completed in MC (see page 45)
1 Basic Cuff completed in CC (see page 46)
232 x 5mm gold color beads
1yd (.95m) decorative ribbon, 1½" (4cm) wide
1 No. 14 "sharp" yarn needle
1 No. 16 beading needle
Sewing thread, to match MC, CC, and/or invisible nylon thread

PATTERNS AND TEMPLATES (STYLE A)

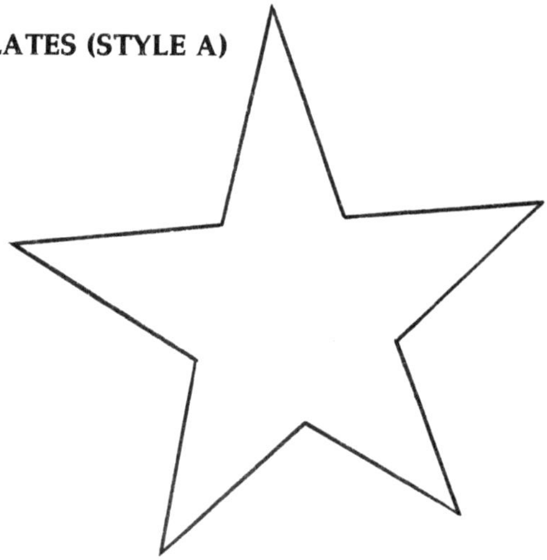

Fig. 3.3 Star Template
(Actual Size)

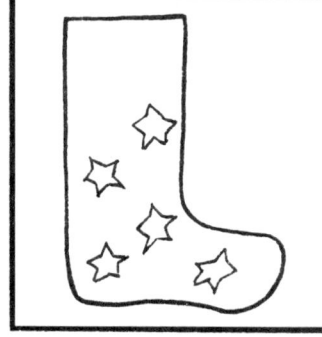

Fig. 3.4 Stocking (Style A)/
Star Placement Guide

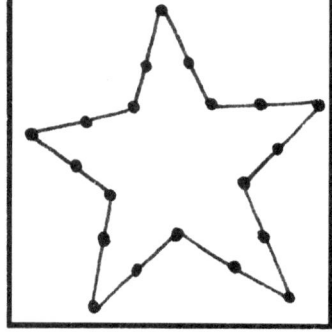

Fig. 3.5 Stocking (Style A)/
Bead Placement Guide (• = 1 bead)

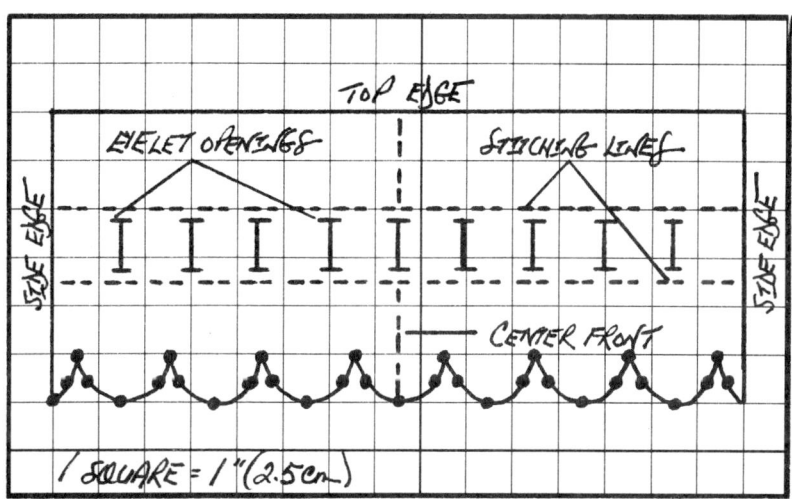

Fig. 3.6 Cuff (Style A)/Scallop Edge Template, Eyelet and Bead Placement Guide (• = 1 bead)

INSTRUCTIONS

1. Trace star pattern (Fig. 3.3, page 48) onto heavy paper and cut out to make a template. On RS of each stocking section, using template and CC thread, baste an outline of the star in each position as shown in Fig. 3.4. With beading needle and invisible thread, attach beads on the basted outline (Fig. 3.5). Remove basting threads.

2. With RS together, join the stocking sections with a flat seam around side and lower edges. Turn stocking to RS.

3. Cuff: With a long machine stitch or hand basting, using CC thread, stitch a line 2" (5cm) below and parallel to top edge of cuff. Stitch a second line 1½" (4cm) below and parallel to first stitched line (Fig. 3.6).

4. Eyelet Openings: At center front of cuff, cut a 1½" (4cm) opening between the stitched lines. Working from center front to each side edge, cut 8 more openings between stitched lines every 1½" (4cm) (Fig. 3.6).

5. Enlarge scallop edge pattern (Fig. 3.6) until grid squares measure 1" (2.5cm). Trace onto heavy paper and cut out to make a template. On RS of cuff, align straight edge of template with top edge of cuff. Cut opposite long edge into

scallop shape. Attach beads on scallop edge (Fig. 3.6).

6. With RS together, join side edges of cuff. Turn cuff to RS. Tunnel RS of cuff to inside (WS) of stocking, aligning top edges and matching cuff seam to back seam of stocking. Join cuff to stocking with a flat seam along top edge. Turn cuff to RS of stocking.

7. Beginning and ending at the eyelet opening at RS of center front of cuff, weave ribbon through eyelets. Tie ribbon in bow at center front.

8. Hanging Loop: With CC yarn, knit a 4" (10cm) cord (see Making A Knitted Cord, page 34). Fold cord in half and join unfolded ends to WS of stocking at back seam, 1" (2.5cm) below top edge.

Style B - Lattice and Beads (See page 41)
MATERIALS
1 Basic Stocking completed in MC (see page 45)
1 Basic Cuff completed in CC (see page 46)
30 x 5mm gold color beads
1yd (.95m) decorative ribbon, 1½" (4cm) wide
3 skeins (each approx 8¾yd/8m) gold metallic embroidery floss
1 No. 14 "sharp" yarn needle
1 No. 16 beading needle
Sewing thread, to match MC, CC, and/or invisible nylon thread

PATTERNS AND TEMPLATES (STYLE B)

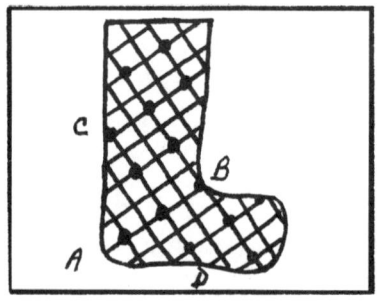

Fig. 3.7 Stocking (Style B)/Stitching Lines and Bead Placement Guide (• = 1 bead)

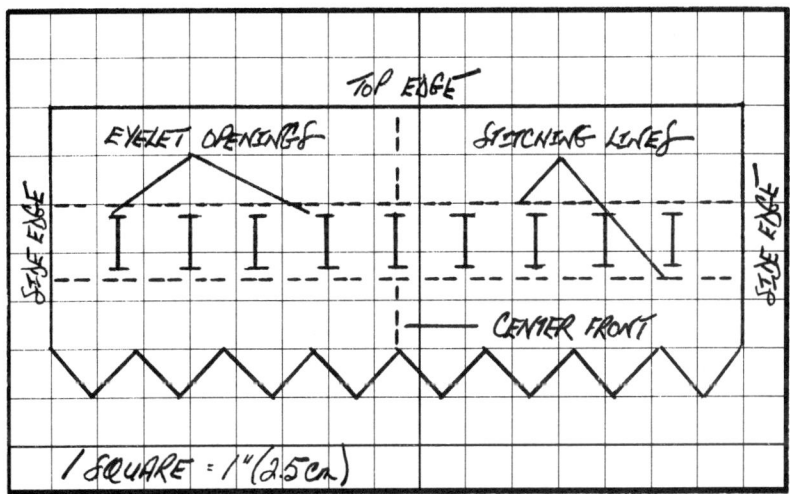

Fig. 3.8 Cuff (Style B)/Zig Zag Edge Template and Eyelet Placement Guide

INSTRUCTIONS

1. On RS of each stocking section, with MC thread and a long machine stitch or hand basting, stitch lines A to B and C to D (Fig. 3.7, page 50). Continue to stitch lines parallel to first lines, 1½" (4cm) apart. With 3 strands of gold metallic embroidery floss, work a back stitch (See An Embroidery Primer, page 32) along all stitched lines on stocking sections. With beading needle and invisible thread, attach beads in position as shown in Fig. 3.7.

2. With RS together, join the stocking sections with a flat seam around side and lower edges. Turn stocking to RS.

3. Cuff: With a long machine stitch or hand basting, using CC thread, stitch a line 2" (5cm) below and parallel to top edge of cuff. Stitch a second line 1½" (4cm) below and parallel to first stitched line (Fig. 3.8)

4. Eyelet Openings: At center front of cuff, cut a 1½" (4cm) opening between the stitched lines. Working from center front to each side edge, cut 8 more openings between stitched lines every 1½" (4cm) (Fig. 3.8)

5. Enlarge zig zag edge pattern (Fig. 3.8) until grid squares measure 1" (2.5cm). Trace onto heavy paper and cut out to make a template. On RS of cuff, align straight edge of

template with top edge of cuff. Cut opposite long edge into zig zag shape.

6. With RS together, join side edges of cuff. Turn cuff to RS. Tunnel RS of cuff to inside (WS) of stocking, aligning top edges and matching cuff seam to back seam of stocking. Join cuff to stocking with a flat seam along top edge. Turn cuff to RS of stocking.

7. Beginning and ending at the eyelet opening at RS of center front of cuff, weave ribbon through eyelets. Tie ribbon in bow at center front.

8. Hanging Loop: With CC yarn, knit a 4" (10cm) of cord (see Making A Knitted Cord, page 34). Fold cord in half and join unfolded ends to WS of stocking at back seam, 1" (2.5cm) below top edge.

Style C - Stars and Lace (See page 41)

MATERIALS

1 Basic Stocking completed in MC (see page 45)
Yarn (to match weight of MC) in CC for cuff (for quantities, see Basic Cuff Chart, page 46)
Yarn (to match weight of MC), in two additional colors (for quantities, see Felted Stars Chart, page 53)
Stitch markers
24 x 5mm gold color beads
1 No. 14 "sharp" yarn needle
1 No. 16 beading needle
Sewing thread, to match MC, CC, and/or invisible nylon thread

PATTERN STITCHES (STYLE C)

Diamond Lace Edging

Row 1: (RS) K to marker, k7, yo, sl 1, k1, psso, yo, k4.

Row 2 and every alt row: K2, p to last 2 sts before marker, k2, p to end.

Row 3: K to marker, k6, (yo, sl 1, k1, psso) twice, yo, k4.

Row 5: K to marker, k5, (yo, sl 1, k1, psso) 3 times, yo, k4.

Row 7: K to marker, k4, (yo, sl 1, k1, psso) 4 times, yo, k4.

Row 9: K to marker, k3, (yo, sl 1, k1, psso) 5 times, yo, k4

Row 11: K to marker, k4, (yo, sl 1, k1, psso) 5 times, k2tog, k2.
Row 13: K to marker, k5, (yo, sl 1, k1, psso) 4 times, k2tog, k2.
Row 15: K to marker, k6, (yo, sl 1, k1, psso) 3 times, k2tog, k2.
Row 17: K to marker, k7, (yo, sl 1, k1, psso) twice, k2tog, k2.
Row 19: K to marker, k8, yo, sl 1, k1, psso, k2tog, k2.
Row 20: As Row 2.
Repeat Rows 1 - 20 for pattern.

INSTRUCTIONS

1. Felted Stars: Refer to the Basic Stocking Chart (page 45) for suggested needle size, knitting gauge and shrinkage percentages for the yarn weight you have chosen. Yarn quantities, knitting instructions and felted measurements are shown in the chart below. Knit and felt *two* pieces (one piece in each color) as instructed.

Felted Stars Chart

Yarn Weight	*Sport*	*Worsted*	*Bulky*
No. of Balls (in each of two colors)	1 (1¾oz/50g) each approx (164yd/150m)	1 (1¾oz/50g) each approx (114yd/104m)	1 (3½oz/100g) each approx (120yd/110m)
Cast on ...	72 sts	54 sts	40 sts
Work in st st ...	68 rows	52 rows	40 rows
Bind off ...	72 sts	54 sts	40 sts
Felted Size WIDTH LENGTH	9½" (24cm) 6¼" (16cm)	9½" (24cm) 6¼" (16cm)	9½" (24cm) 6¼" (16cm)

2. Trace star pattern (Fig. 3.3, page 48) onto heavy paper and cut out to make a template. From each felted piece, cut six stars and position three of each color on RS of each stocking section (Fig. 3.9, page 54). With beading needle and invisible thread, join each star to stocking with a bead at center of star.

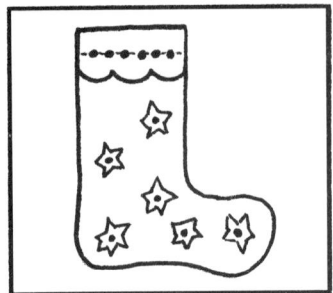

Fig. 3.9 Stocking and Cuff (Style C)/Star and Bead Placement Guide
(• = 1 bead)

3. With RS together, join the stocking sections with a flat seam around side and lower edges. Turn stocking to RS.
4. Cuff: Refer to the Basic Cuff Chart (page 46) for yarn quantities, suggested needle size, knitting gauge and shrinkage percentages for the yarn weight you have chosen. Knit and felt one cuff as instructed in the Lace Cuff Chart below.

Lace Cuff Chart

Yarn Weight	*Sport*	*Worsted*	*Bulky*
Cast on ... Place stitch marker on needle Cast on ...	13 sts 33 sts	13 sts 21 sts	13 sts 11 sts
Work in Diamond Lace Edging (see page 52) ...	160 rows	120 rows	100 rows
Bind off ...	46 sts	34 sts	24 sts
Felted Size WIDTH LENGTH	6" (15cm) 15" (38cm)	6" (15cm) 15" (38cm)	6" (15cm) 15" (38cm)

5. Attach 12 beads to cuff (Fig. 3.9). With RS together, join side edges of cuff. Turn cuff to RS. Tunnel RS of cuff to inside (WS) of stocking, aligning top edges and matching cuff seam to back seam of stocking. Join cuff to stocking with a flat seam along top edge. Turn cuff to RS of stocking.
6. Hanging Loop: With CC yarn, knit a 4" (10cm) cord (see Making A Knitted Cord, page 34). Fold cord in half and join unfolded ends to WS of stocking at back seam, 1" (2.5cm) below top edge.

Style D - Fringe and Tinsel (See page 41)
MATERIALS
1 Basic Stocking, one side completed in MC and one side completed in CC (see page 45)
1 Basic Cuff completed in MC (see page 46)
3yd (2.7m) gold color decorative cording, ¼" (7mm) wide
2 skeins (each approx 8¾yd/8m) gold metallic embroidery floss
Crochet hook
1 No. 14 "sharp" yarn needle
Sewing thread, to match MC, CC, and/or invisible nylon thread

PATTERNS AND TEMPLATES (STYLE D)

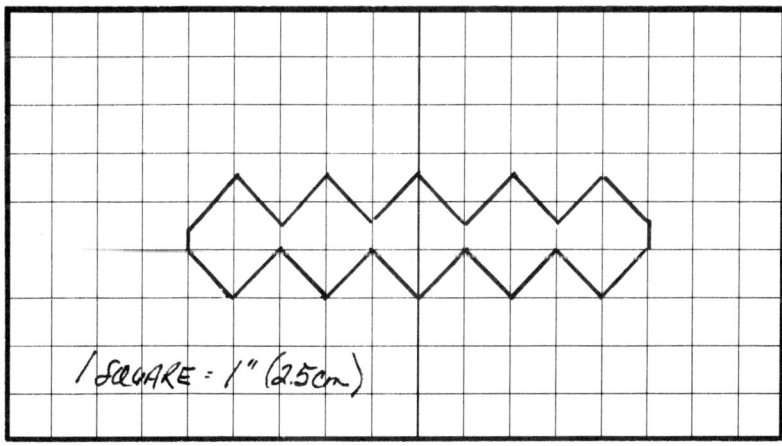

/ SQUARE = / " (2.5cm)

Fig. 3.10 Stocking (Style D)/Zig Zag Template

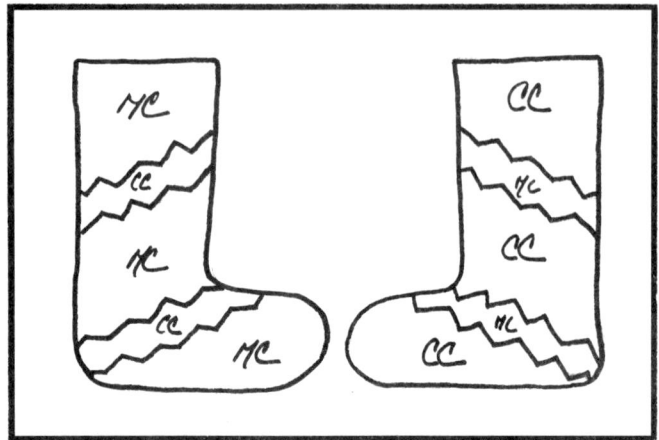

Fig. 3.11 Stocking (Style D)/Zig Zag Placement Guide

INSTRUCTIONS

1. Enlarge zig zag pattern (Fig. 3.10) until grid squares measure 1" (2.5cm). Trace onto heavy paper and cut out to make a template. With RS of each stocking section facing up, place the zig zag template (RS up) onto stocking as shown in Fig. 3.11. Cut out two zig zag sections from each stocking section. Interchange these four zig zag strips so that two MC strips are on the CC stocking side and two CC strips are on the MC stocking side. With matching or invisible thread, on the WS, join the zig zag sections to stocking to make each side complete (see Seams, page 31). On RS, outline each zig zag section with gold cording. Join cording using invisible thread and overcast stitch.

2. With RS together, join the stocking sections with a flat seam around side and lower edges. Turn stocking to RS.

3. Cuff: With RS together, join side edges of cuff. Turn cuff to RS. Tunnel RS of cuff to inside (WS) of stocking, aligning top edges and matching cuff seam to back seam of stocking. Join cuff to stocking with a flat seam along top edge. Turn cuff to RS of stocking.

4. Cuff Fringe: Make 20 fringes in a finished length of 2" (5cm), each with four strands of CC yarn and four strands of gold

metallic embroidery floss (see Beyond The Fringe, page 35). With crochet hook, join each fringe evenly around lower edge of cuff. Trim finished fringe to an even length.
5. Hanging Loop: With MC yarn, knit a 4" (10cm) cord (see Making A Knitted Cord, page 34). Fold cord in half and join unfolded ends to WS of stocking at back seam, 1" (2.5cm) below top edge.

Style E - Eyelet and Ribbons (See page 41)
MATERIALS
1 Basic Stocking completed in MC (see page 45)   To create the decorative edge, cut out stocking pattern (Fig. 3.2, page 47) with a rotary cutter using a "wave" or a "pinking" blade
1 Basic Cuff completed in CC (see page 46)
1yd (.95m) each of ¼" (7mm) wide decorative ribbon, in three colors
1 No. 14 "sharp" yarn needle
Sewing thread, to match MC, CC, and/or invisible nylon thread

PATTERNS AND TEMPLATES (STYLE E)

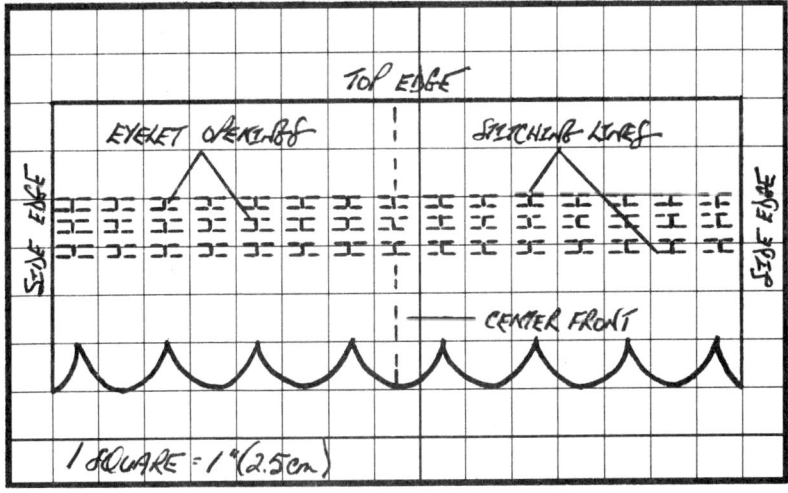

Fig. 3.12 Cuff (Style E)/Scallop Edge Template and Eyelet Placement Guide

INSTRUCTIONS

1. With WS together, join the stocking sections around side and lower edges by working a ¼" (7mm) length back stitch (see An Embroidery Primer, page 32) in CC yarn with the stitching line ½" (12mm) from cut edge.

2. Cuff: With a long machine stitch or hand basting, using CC thread, stitch a line 2" (5cm) below and parallel to top edge of cuff. Stitch five more lines, ¼" (7mm) apart and parallel to the to first stitched line (Fig. 3.12).

3. Eyelet Openings: At center front of cuff, cut a ¼" (7mm) opening between the first and second, third and fourth, and fifth and sixth stitched lines. Working from center front to each side edge, cut 14 more openings every 1" (2.5cm) between stitched lines (Fig. 3.12).

4. Enlarge scallop edge pattern (Fig. 3.12) until grid squares measure 1" (2.5cm). Trace pattern onto heavy paper and cut out to make a template. On RS of cuff, align straight edge of template with top edge of cuff. Cut opposite long edge into scallop shape.

5. With RS together, join side edges of cuff. Turn cuff to RS. Tunnel RS of cuff to inside (WS) of stocking, aligning top edges and matching cuff seam to back seam of stocking. Join cuff to stocking with a flat seam along top edge. Turn cuff to RS of stocking.

6. Beginning and ending at the eyelet opening on RS of center front of cuff, weave one color of ribbon through each row of eyelets. Tie each ribbon in bow at center front.

7. Hanging Loop: With CC yarn, knit a 4" (10cm) cord (see Making A Knitted Cord, page 34). Fold cord in half and join unfolded ends to WS of stocking at back seam, 1" (2.5cm) below top edge.

A Felted Christmas Tree Skirt

When we bring the Christmas tree into our homes, whether it is of the natural or artificial variety, we pay most of our attention to decorating the boughs and branches, finally topping the tree with a special angel figure or memento. This year make a tree skirt to add that finishing touch. The stencil-like motif of angels and stars ensures that your tree will be surrounded by heavenly guardians.

The project instructions that follow will guide you in completing the tree skirt as shown on page 41. You can add your own creativity by varying the yarn weights and color combinations.

FINISHED SIZE
The finished size for the tree skirt is the measurement after felting the knitting and assembly of the skirt.
Finished diameter of tree skirt
36" (92cm)

MATERIALS
The yarn amounts listed in the Tree Skirt Chart (see page 61), are what you will need, in a selected yarn weight of a 100% animal fiber, to complete the six background sections of the skirt, three each of Col A (green) and Col B (blue).

The additional yarn amounts listed below are what you will need to complete the motif patterns and knitted cord.

No. of Balls	Sport	Worsted	Bulky
Col A (green)	1½	1½	1
Col B (blue)	1½	1½	1
Col C (yellow)	1½	1½	1
Col D (rose)	2	3	2
Cols E, F, and G	½	½	½

(white, purple, gold)
In addition, you will need:
132 x 6mm wooden beads
1 No. 14 "sharp" yarn needle
1 No. 16 beading needle
Sewing thread, to match Col A, Col B, and/or invisible nylon thread

GAUGE

Knit a large sample, in the yarn weight you have chosen, at least 8" (20cm) square, to test both knitting gauge and felting shrinkage, as listed in the Tree Skirt Chart (page 61).

(See Knitting Your Sample, page 13 and Felting Your Knitted Sample, page 24)

SHRINKAGE PERCENTAGES

$\dfrac{\text{Gauge Before Felting}}{\text{Gauge After Felting}}$ x 100% = Percentage of Shrinkage

Example (using worsted weight yarn):

Stitch Gauge:				Row Gauge:			
$\dfrac{20}{22.5}$	x	100	= 88%	$\dfrac{26}{33}$	x	100	= 79%

These are the percentages of shrinkage that must occur during the felting of the knitted sample in order to obtain the correct finished size.

The felted sample should be 88% of the width and 79% of the length of the knitted sample *before* felting.

INSTRUCTIONS

1. Tree Skirt Sections: Follow the Tree Skirt Chart (page 61) and knit *six* pieces, three in each of Col A (green) and Col B (blue). Felt the knitted pieces to obtain felted measurements as listed. Enlarge the Tree Skirt Pattern (Fig. 3.14, page 62) until grid squares measure 1" (2.5cm). From each felted piece (RS up), cut one skirt section.

2. Stencil Motifs: Refer to the Tree Skirt Chart for suggested needle size, knitting gauge and felting shrinkage. Follow the Stencil Motif Chart (page 63) to complete the knitted pieces. Felt the knitted pieces to obtain felted measurements as listed. Enlarge the Stencil Motif Patterns (Fig. 3.14) until grid squares measure 1" (2.5cm). Trace these patterns and star pattern (Fig. 3.3, page 48) onto heavy paper and cut out to make templates.

3. From the felted pieces, cut out the following:
   Col A (green) - 3 angel bodies

(continued on page 63)

Tree Skirt Chart

Yarn Weight	*Sport*	*Worsted*	*Bulky*
No. of Balls Col A (green) Col B (blue)	8 (1¾oz/50g) 8 (1¾oz/50g) each approx (164yd/150m)	7 (1¾oz/50g) 7 (1¾oz/50g) each approx (114yd/104m)	5 (3½oz/100g) 5 (3½oz/100g) each approx (120yd/110m)
Needle Size (suggested)	3.75mm (CAN9/US5)	4.5mm (CAN7/US7)	6mm (CAN4/US10)
Knitting Gauge (4"/10cm over st st)	24 sts x30 rows	20 sts x 26 rows	14 sts x20 rows
Shrinkage %: (approximate) WIDTH LENGTH	80% 70%	88% 79%	86% 82%
Cast on ...	154 sts	120 sts	84 sts
Work in st st, dec 1 st each edge every 3rd row ...	58 times	45 times	31 times
Work even in st st ...	26 rows	15 rows	19 rows
Bind off ...	38 sts	30 sts	22 sts
Felted Size (Fig. 3.13, page 62) A B C	5" (13cm) 18" (46cm) 20" (51cm)	5" (13cm) 18" (46cm) 20" (51cm)	5" (13cm) 18" (46cm) 20" (51cm)

Fig. 3.13 Felted Measurement Guide for Tree Skirt Section

A
B
C

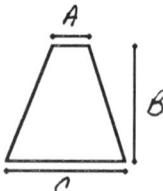

Fig. 3.14 Tree Skirt Section and Stencil Motif Patterns (• = 1 bead)

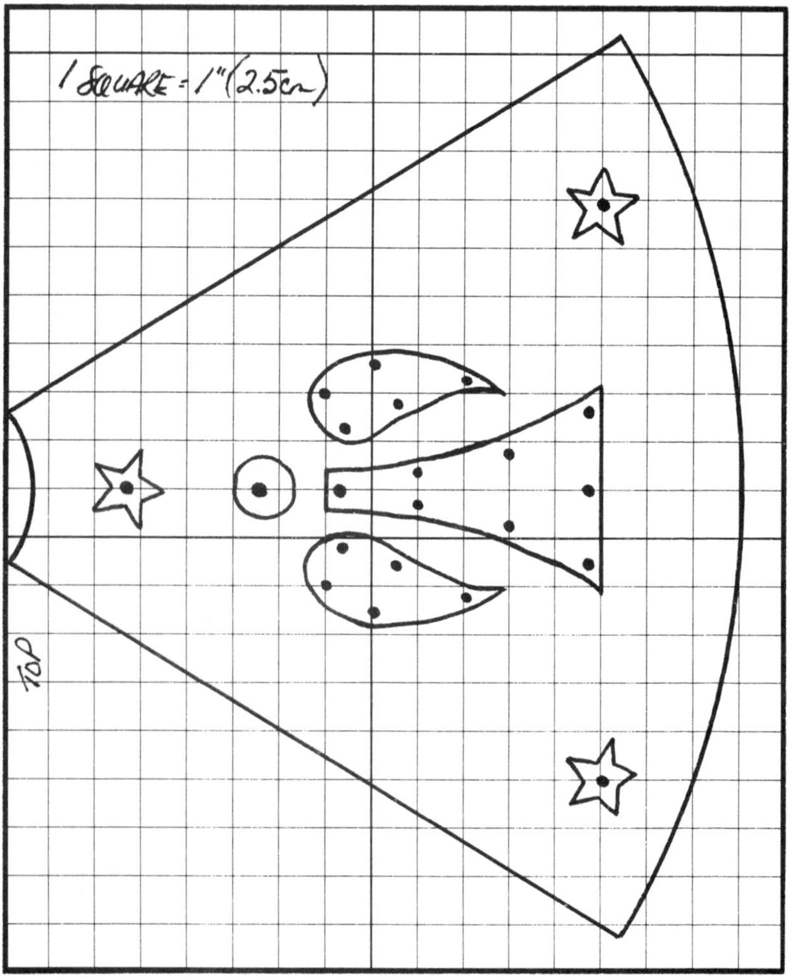

1 SQUARE = 1" (2.5cm)
TOP

Stencil Motif Chart

Yarn Weight	*Sport*	*Worsted*	*Bulky*
Work in st st ...			
Col A (green)	134 sts x 78 rows	104 sts x 60 rows	72 sts x 44 rows
Col B (blue)	134 sts x 78 rows	104 sts x 60 rows	72 sts x 44 rows
Col C (yellow)	60 sts x 154 rows	46 sts x 120 rows	32 sts x 88 rows
Col D (rose)	42 sts x 46 rows	32 sts x 34 rows	24 sts x 26 rows
Cols E, F, and G (white, purple, gold)	60 sts x 52 rows	46 sts x 40 rows	32 sts x 30 rows
Felted Size *(WIDTH x LENGTH)*			
Col A	(17¾ x 7)" (45 x 18)cm	(17¾ x 7)" (45 x 18)cm	(17¾ x 7)" (45 x 18)cm
Col B	(17¾ x 7)" (45 x 18)cm	(17¾ x 7)" (45 x 18)cm	(17¾ x 7)" (45 x 18)cm
Col C	(8 x 14¼)" (20 x 36)cm	(8 x 14¼)" (20 x 36)cm	(8 x 14¼)" (20 x 36)cm
Col D	(5½ x 4)" (14 x 10)cm	(5½ x 4)" (14 x 10)cm	(5½ x 4)" (14 x 10)cm
Cols E, F, and G	(8 x 4¾)" (20 x 12)cm	(8 x 4¾)" (20 x 12)cm	(8 x 4¾)" (20 x 12)cm

(continued from page 60)

Col B (blue) - 3 angel bodies
Col C (yellow) - 12 wings (6 with RS of pattern down)
Col D (rose) - 6 angel heads
Cols E, F, and G - 6 stars of each color
With beading needle and invisible thread, join pattern pieces to each skirt section, (Col A body on a Col B skirt section and Col B body on a Col A skirt section), placing beads as shown in Fig. 3.14.

4. With RS together and a flat seam, alternating Col A (green) and Col B (blue), join the skirt sections along straight sides, leaving one seam open. Turn to RS and press seams *lightly*.

5. Knitted Cords: With Col D (rose), knit seven, 15¼" (39cm)

lengths of cord, (See Making a Knitted Cord, page 34). (Note: The knitted cords are *not* felted.) Press these cords *lightly* to lie flat. Place one length of cord along each skirt seam and one along each side of opening edges. With matching yarn and slip stitch, join cords to skirt.

6. With Col D (rose), knit two cords, one, 44" (112cm) and one, 144" (365cm). Place the shorter length around the top edge of the skirt and the longer length around the lower edge, leaving 12" (30cm) of cord at each end for ties. With Col D (rose), knit two cords, 12" (30cm) each, and join one to each opening edge 7½" (19cm) down from top edge. Join the ties in bows.

A Felted Christmas Hanging

The following felting project will create a wonderful seasonal hanging to place on your front door or over your fireplace. Start by knitting the different colors and textures, then felt to create a "fabric". Cut out the pattern pieces and begin to create a winter scene that wishes everyone who sees it, "Happy Holidays!" (See page 41)

FINISHED SIZE
The finished size for the seasonal hanging is the measurement after felting and assembly of the felted pieces.
Finished measurement of hanging (including border)
(21½ x 21½)" or (55 x 55)cm

MATERIALS
Yarn amounts required, in a selected yarn weight of 100% animal fiber, are listed below. Refer to the Felted Hanging Chart (page 67) for yardage amounts per ball for individual yarn weights.

No. of Balls	Sport	Worsted	Bulky
Col A (white)	2	2	1
Col B (mauve)	2	2	1
Col C (blue)	1	1	1
Col D (red)	1	1	1
Col G (dark green)	1	1	1
Col H (light green)	1	1	1

(continued from page 66)

5. House Assembly: With Col J (khaki green) and back stitch (see An Embroidery Primer, page 32), work frames on window sections and molding on the door section (Fig. 3.15, page 69). On house section, with a contrast color thread, baste an outline of the windows and door. Cut along stitched lines to create openings. Working on WS with a flat seam, join windows and door into openings (see Seams, page 31). With a flat seam, join top edge of path to lower edge of door and lower edges of chimneys to top edge of roof (placing one chimney at each end). With a flat seam, join lower edge of roof to top edge of house. Center house and attached pieces on background so that lower edge of path is even with lower edge of background. With matching yarn and blanket stitch (see An Embroidery Primer, page 32), join house, roof, chimneys and path to background.

6. With matching yarn, join trees to background, (2 large and 1 small tree on each side of house) by working a large single cross stitch in the center of each tree section. Cut the length of Col J (khaki green) felted piece into six even lengths. With matching yarn, join tree trunks to background (one at each base of a tree) with a large cross stitch. With matching yarn, join fence bars to background on each side of house, working a large cross stitch where bars cross.

7. Braid three 20" (51cm) lengths of gold metallic embroidery floss. Tie the braid in a bow and attach to wreath. Join wreath to front door.

8. Enlarge the Felted Hanging Greeting (Fig. 3.16, page 69) until grid squares measure ¼" (7mm) and trace onto tissue paper or lightweight interfacing. Pin the tracing in desired position on the background. With embroidery floss and back stitch, using tracing as a guide, embroider greeting onto background. Cut away traced guide. Join stars to background with whip stitch (see An Embroidery Primer, page 32), worked on all edges.

9. Border: Refer to Felted Hanging Chart (page 67) for suggested needle size, knitting gauge and felting shrinkage. Each length of border begins with a Col D (red) section and ends with a

(continued on page 70)

Felted Hanging Chart

Yarn Weight	*Sport*	*Worsted*	*Bulky*
Yardage per ball (See MATERIALS for no. of balls)	(1¾oz/50g) each approx (164yd/150m)	(1¾oz/50g) each approx (114yd/104m)	(3½oz/100g) each approx (120yd/110m)
Needle Size (suggested)	3.75mm (CAN9/US5)	4.5mm (CAN7/US7)	6mm (CAN4/US10)
Knitting Gauge	24 sts x 30 rows	20 sts x 26 rows	14 sts x 20 rows
Shrinkage %: (approximate) *WIDTH* *LENGTH*	 80% 70%	 88% 79%	 86% 82%
Work in st st ... (in each color) Cols A and B Col C Col H Cols E, G, and J Work in Patt A .. Col D Work in Patt B .. Col F	 138 sts x 96 rows 60 sts x 66 rows 60 sts x 128rows 46 sts x 66 rows 76 sts x 46 rows 62 sts x 86 rows	 104 sts x 75 rows 46 sts x 58 rows 46 sts x 112rows 34 sts x 50 rows 56 sts x 34 rows 46 sts x 66 rows	 76 sts x 56 rows 33 sts x 36 rows 34 sts x 70 rows 24 sts x 36 rows 40 sts x 24 rows 40 sts x 50 rows
Felted Size WIDTH X LENGTH (in each color) Cols A and B Col C Col H Cols E, G, and J Col D Col F	 (18 x 9)" (46 x 23)cm (8 x 6)" (20 x 15)cm (8 x 12)" (20 x 30)cm (6 x 6)" (15 x 15)cm (10 x 4)" (25 x 10)cm (8 x 8)" (20 x 20)cm	 (18 x 9)" (46 x 23)cm (8 x 6)" (20 x 15)cm (8 x 12)" (20 x 30)cm (6 x 6)" (15 x 15)cm (10 x 4)" (25 x 10)cm (8 x 8)" (20 x 20)cm	 (18 x 9)" (46 x 23)cm (8 x 6)" (20 x 15)cm (8 x 12)" (20 x 30)cm (6 x 6)" (15 x 15)cm (10 x 4)" (25 x 10)cm (8 x 8)" (20 x 20)cm

Fig. 3.15 Felted Hanging Patterns

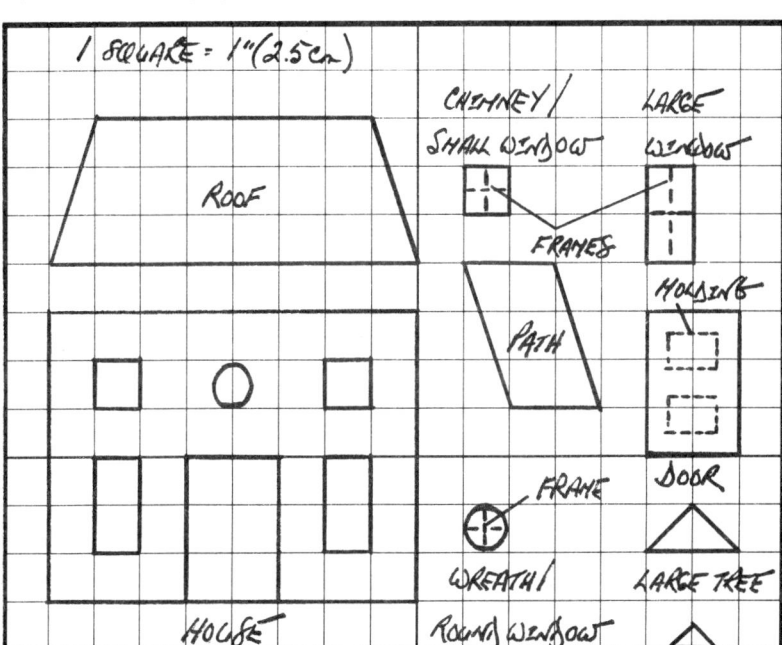

Fig. 3.16 Felted Hanging Greeting

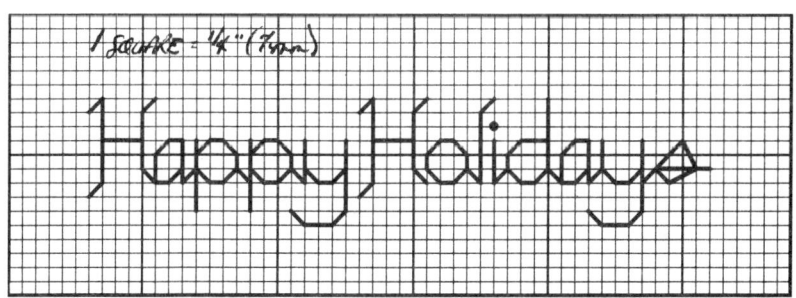

(continued from page 68)

Col G (dark green) section, using lengths of yarn (in colors matching those used in the hanging) to knit the "triangles" in the Border Graph (Fig. 3.17) (Note: The symbols used in the graph are to indicate a *change* in color and do not represent a specific color.) Follow the Felted Hanging Border Chart (page 71) and knit four lengths of the border. Felt the knitted pieces to obtain felted measurements. At each end of each length, cut the Col D (red) and Col G (dark green) sections on the diagonal (these will be joined to create a mitered corner). On the WS and with a flat seam, join one length of border to each side of hanging, placing a Col D (red) and a Col G (dark green) section to meet at each corner. Join the diagonal ends at corners.

10. With Col D (red) and a whip stitch (See An Embroidery Primer, page 32), work around all edges of the four hanging tabs. Fold tabs in half and join unfolded ends to WS of hanging at the border seam of top edge, placing one tab at each end and two placed evenly between.

11. Cut out a piece of fabric for backing, (22½ x 22½)" or (57x 57)cm. Turn under ½" (12mm) on all edges to WS and press. Join WS of backing to WS of hanging, matching edges and enclosing lower edges of the tabs.

12. Slip the wooden dowel through the tabs and glue one finial to each end. For hanging, tie a decorative cord at each end of the dowel.

Fig. 3.17 Border Graph

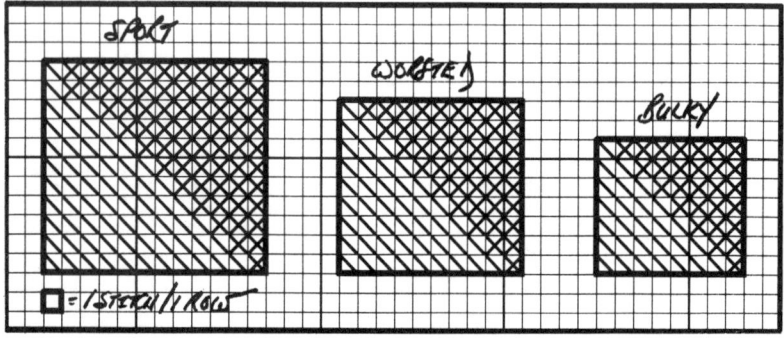

Felted Border Chart

Yarn Weight	*Sport*	*Worsted*	*Bulky*
With Col D (red), cast on...	12 sts	10 sts	8 sts
Work in st st ...	12 rows	10 rows	8 rows
Work from graph (page 70) repeating ...	Rows 1 - 11	Rows 1 - 9	Rows 1 - 7
for ...	24 times	22 times	22 times
With Col G (dark green), work in st st ...	12 rows	10 rows	8 rows
Bind off ...	12 sts	10 sts	8 sts
Felted Size WIDTH X LENGTH	(1½ x 24½)" (4 x 62)cm	(1½ x 24½)" (4 x 62)cm	(1½ x 24½)" (4 x 62)cm

PART FOUR
Heartfelt Presents

is heartfelt presents
lt presents heartfel
ts heartfelt present
presents heartfelt p
sents heartfelt pres
artfelt presents hea
ts heartfelt present
resents heartfelt pr
presents heartfelt
felt presents heartf
heartfelt presents h
s heartfelt presents
nts heartfelt presen

CLOCKWISE FROM TOP LEFT:
Felted teddy bears, knit plain or in plaid. Bookmarks. Three sizes of gift bags, striped, embroidered and tasseled. Sachets (below), in small pillows, star, heart and butterfly shapes. Felted bags (below left). Shell-motif cases and purses (left).

Heartfelt Presents

We try to do our best when choosing a gift for someone. We want it to be the right offering - always attractive and perhaps useful. Our gifts represent us, particularly if it is something we have made ourselves. It shows off a creative ability that is unique to each one of us. The expressions of those talents tell others of our special gifts and our wish to share them.

A handmade gift is by no doubt the most honest and loving. It is not only a result of your special creativity but requires an element that is so precious to all of us - our time and energy. Taking time in our fast-paced world to fashion a special item, is a true gift reserved for those cherished few in our lives.

In this section, there are a dozen choices that will add up to a felted teddy bear of different sizes, dressed up in a plain or a plaid suit. There are bottle bags and jar bags ready to present one of your house specialties in a pretty enclosure or felted bags with ribbons and tassels to hold unknown treasures. There are cedar-scented sachets, cut out in fanciful shapes, which will make great stocking stuffers (not to mention keeping pests away from stored woolen items). Finally, you will find practical givings of eyeglass cases, small purses, and bookmarks to help to check off everyone on your list.

Teddy Bears Do Wear Plaid

Don't restrict your teddy bear giving to the young ones on your gift list. Anyone could benefit from a hug or two with such a cuddly companion.

Following you will find instructions for two sizes of teddy bears. Multiply these two sizes by the three yarn weights, decide whether you wish to knit it plain (with contrast color paws and ears) or in a plaid pattern, and you will find that you have a dozen choices of teddy bears. (See page 75)

If you are making this bear for a young child, even though the recommended eyes and nose have a safety lock, take the extra time to embroider the facial features. This will guarantee that the teddy can handle lots of safe and carefree hugs.

Felted Teddy Bear

SIZES

Instructions are given for the small size, with the large size in parentheses. If one instruction is given, it applies to both sizes.

Small (Large)

FINISHED SIZES

The finished size is the measurement after felting the knitted pieces and assembly of the teddy bear.

Finished length of teddy bear (from head to toe)

Yarn Weight	Sport	Worsted	Bulky
Small	11¾" (30cm)	14¼" (36cm)	18" (46cm)
Large	15" (38cm)	16½" (42cm)	22" (56cm)

MATERIALS

The yarn amounts listed in the Teddy Bear Chart (see page 79) are what you will need, in a selected yarn weight of a 100% animal fiber, to complete each teddy bear.

In addition, you will need:

Length of black yarn, to embroider mouth

1 No. 14 "sharp" yarn needle

1 pair ½" (12mm) safety-lock eyes

1, ¾" (20mm) safety-lock nose

1 lb (454g) polyester fiberfill

1 yd (.95m) decorative ribbon, 1" (2.5cm) wide

GAUGE

Knit a large sample (plaid pattern for plaid bear), in the yarn weight you have chosen, at least 8" (20cm) square, to test both knitting gauge and felting shrinkage, as listed in the Teddy Bear Chart. (See Knitting Your Sample, page 13 and Felting Your Knitted Sample, page 24)

SHRINKAGE PERCENTAGES

$$\frac{\text{Gauge Before Felting}}{\text{Gauge After Felting}} \times 100\% = \text{Percentage of Shrinkage}$$

Example (using worsted weight yarn):

(continued on page 79)

Teddy Bear Chart

Yarn Weight	*Sport*	*Worsted*	*Bulky*
Yardage per ball	(1¾oz/50g) each approx (164yd/150m)	(1¾oz/50g) each approx (114yd/104m)	(3½oz/100g) each approx (120yd/110m)
No. of Balls SMALL (LARGE) SIZE **Plain Bear** Col A Col B **Plaid Bear** Col A Col B Col C	4 (5) 1 (1) 8 (9) 4 (4) 1 (1)	3 (4) 1 (1) 7 (8) 3 (3) 1 (1)	3 (4) 1 (1) 6 (7) 2 (2) 1 (1)
Needle Size (suggested)	3.75mm (CAN9/US5)	4.5mm (CAN7/US7)	6mm (CAN4/US10)
Knitting Gauge	24 sts x 30 rows	20 sts x 26 rows	14 sts x 20 rows
Shrinkage %: (approximate) *WIDTH* *LENGTH*	80% 70%	88% 79%	86% 82%
Felted Size (LENGTH OF BEAR) Small Large	11¾" (30cm) 15" (38cm)	14¼" (36cm) 16½" (42cm)	18" (46cm) 22" (56cm)

(continued from page 78)

Stitch Gauge: Row Gauge:

$$\frac{20}{22.5} \times 100 = 88\% \qquad \frac{26}{33} \times 100 = 79\%$$

These are the percentages of shrinkage that must occur during the felting of the knitted sample in order to obtain the correct finished size.

The felted sample should be 88% of the width and 79% of the length of the knitted sample *before* felting.

INSTRUCTIONS

Note 1: Increases and decreases are worked on the second stitch of the row and on the second to last stitch of the row (see page 16). Pieces knit in "reverse" are worked in the same direction but with the increases or decreases worked on opposite sides.

Note 2: When knitting the plaid pattern and using two colors in one row, twist colors to avoid creating holes in your work. When knitting the vertical plaid stripe, use separate lengths of yarn and do not carry yarn across the row.

Note 3: When working the duplicate stitch in Col C, continue the duplicate stitch over the knitted plaid sections every second stitch or row as shown on graphs.

Note 4: All seams are worked with RS together and flat seam, unless instructed otherwise.

1. Knit all teddy bear pieces in stocking (stockinette) stitch from the graphs (pages 81 to 83), working in the direction of the arrow and following the outline for the small or large size. Label each piece of the knitting to avoid confusion.

    Arms: Knit 4 pieces in Col A (or plaid pattern), 2 reversed.

    Legs: Knit 4 pieces in Col A (or plaid pattern), 2 reversed.

    Body Front: Knit 2 pieces in Col A (or plaid pattern), 1 reversed.

    Body Back: Knit 2 pieces in Col A (or plaid pattern), 1 reversed.

    Head Side: Knit 2 pieces in Col A (or plaid pattern), 1 reversed.

    Center Head: Knit 1 piece in Col A (or plaid pattern).

    Ear: Knit 4 pieces, 2 in Col A, 2 in Col B.

    Paw Pads: Knit 2 pieces in Col B.

    Foot Pads: Knit 2 pieces in Col B.

2. If making the plaid pattern, work duplicate stitch (see Duplicate Stitch/Swiss Darning, page 17) on knitted pieces, *before* felting. Felt the knitted pieces.

3. Arms: On RS at lower edge of each inner arm, with Col B slip stitch a paw pad to lower edge, matching curves. With RS together and Col A, join inner arm to outer arm, leaving open at shoulder. Turn to RS and stuff each arm firmly.

(continued on page 83)

Fig. 4.1 Teddy Bear Graph Legend

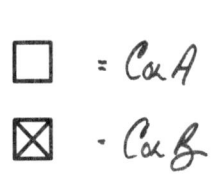

☐ = Col A

☒ · Col B

◺ · Col C

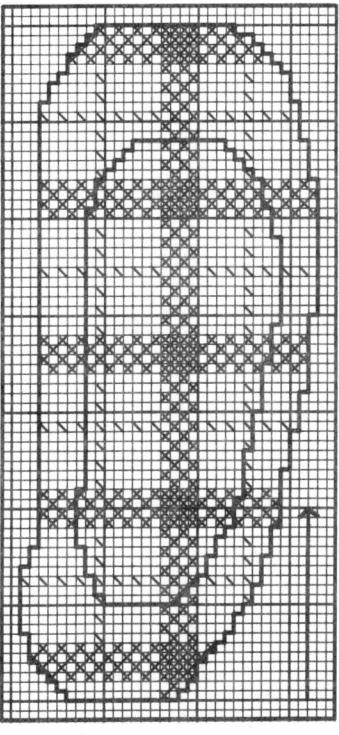

Arm

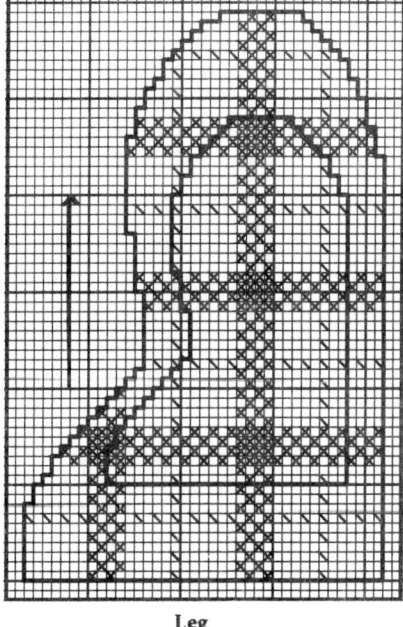

Leg

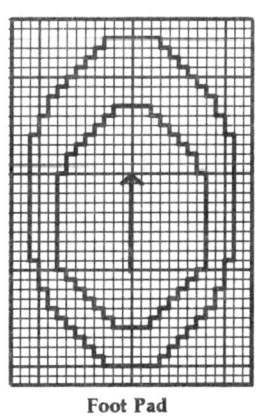

Foot Pad

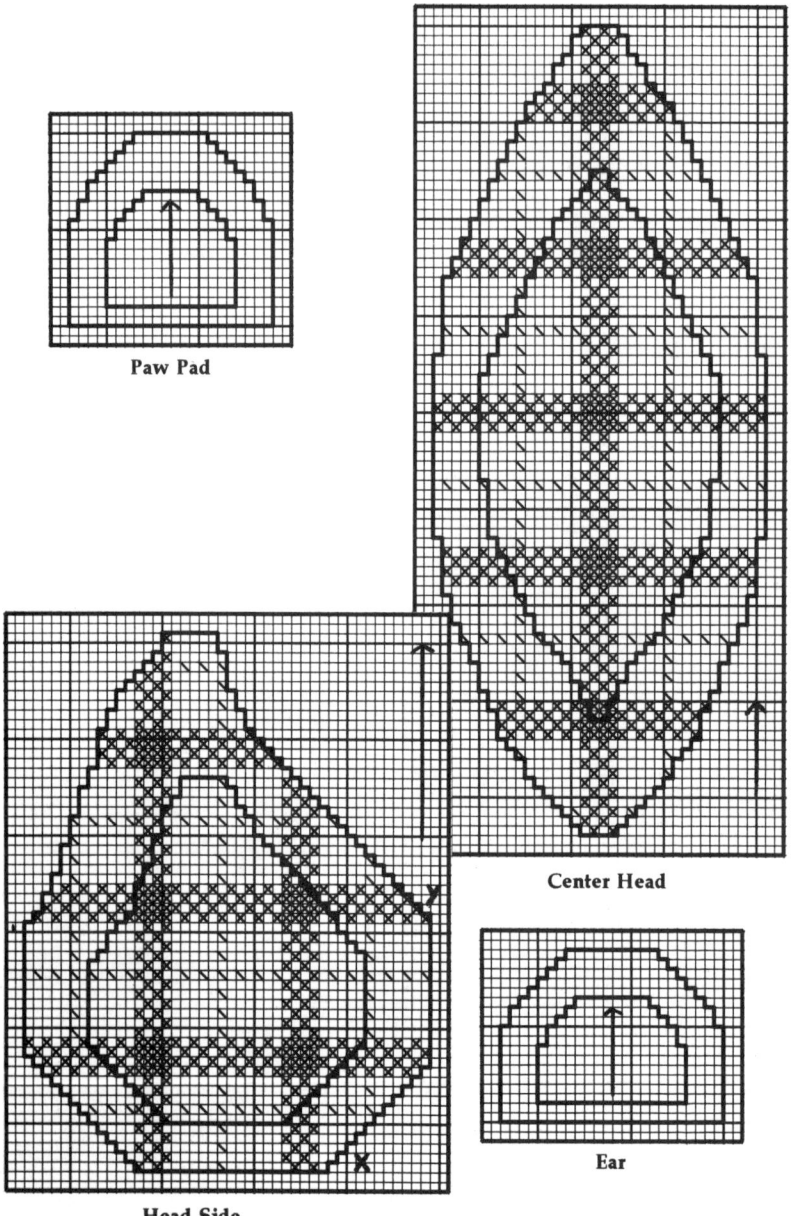

Paw Pad

Center Head

Ear

Head Side

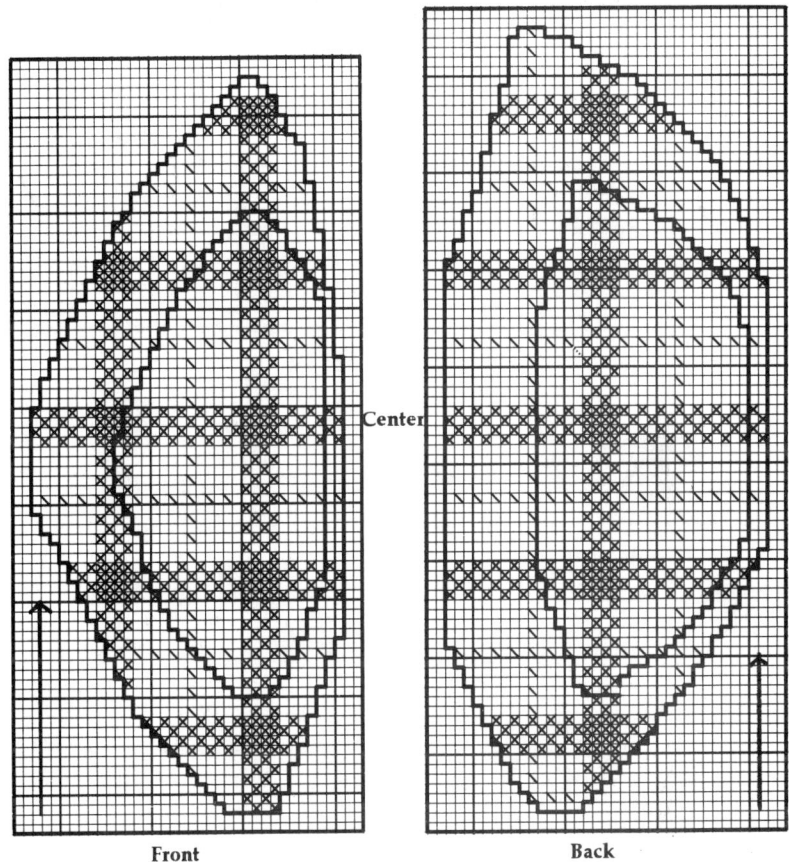

Front   Back

(continued from page 80)

4. Legs: With RS together and Col A, join front and back sections of legs at side seams, leaving open at top. Turn to RS. With Col B, slip stitch a foot pad to larger opening (bottom of leg), matching edges. Stuff each leg firmly, shaping thighs with extra fiberfill.

5. Body: With RS together and Col A, join fronts at center seam. With RS together and Col A, join body front to body back sections at side seams. Join center back seam, leaving a small opening. Turn to RS and stuff body firmly. Close opening with a slip stitch.

6. Head: With RS together and Col A, join the two side head pieces, beginning at front neck opening to top of snout (X to Y on head side graph). Join each side head to center head, beginning at back neck opening to snout, and down the other side to back neck opening. Turn head to RS and stuff firmly. Attach nose to top of snout with safety lock. With a double strand of black yarn, embroider mouth, working one vertical and two horizontal stitches. Position eyes, for desired expression and add safety lock. With Col A, run a gathering stitch around neck opening, pull slightly so that lower edge of head is evenly gathered. Place head on body (face to the front) and tack in place, adding extra stuffing to keep neck firm.

7. Tack tops of arms and legs to body, so that bear is in a sitting position. Add extra stuffing as needed. With Col A and an overcast stitch, join all seams as tacked. Repeat, to ensure that all seams are secure.

8. Ears: With RS together and Col B, join a Col A ear section (back of ear) to a Col B ear section around curved edge, leaving bottom edge open. Turn ears to RS. With Col A, work a small backstitch around curve, ¼" (7mm) from edge, to create a solid ridge around top of each ear. Join bottom edges of ears, gathering slightly. Pin ears into position on head and sew firmly with an overcast stitch. Tie ribbon in bow around neck.

Felted Bags

A felted bag makes the perfect carrier for a bottle of flavored vinegar or a jar of homemade pickles. Three sizes of gift bags with their secrets sealed by a tassel or bow, can create a soft surround for a delicate gift. (See page 75)

Bottle Bags
SIZES
Instructions are given for the small size, with the large size in parentheses. If one instruction is given, it applies to all sizes.
Small (Large)

FINISHED SIZES
The finished size is the measurement <u>after</u> felting the knitted pieces and assembly of the bag.
Finished height

Small	**Large**
8" (20cm)	12" (30.5cm)

MATERIALS
The yarn amounts listed in the Bottle Bag Chart (see page 86) are what you will need, in a selected yarn weight of 100% animal fiber, to complete one bottle bag. If knitting in stripe pattern, choose lengths of yarn in complementary colors of matching yarn weights. In addition, you will need:

Rotary blade cutter, with "wave" or "pinking" blade (optional)
1 No. 14 "sharp" yarn needle
1yd (.95m) decorative ribbon, 1½" (4cm) wide
Sewing thread, to match MC and/or invisible nylon thread

GAUGE
Knit a large sample, in the yarn weight you have chosen, at least 8" (20cm) square, to test both knitting gauge and felting shrinkage, as listed in the Bottle Bag Chart.
(See Knitting Your Sample, page 13 and Felting Your Knitted Sample, page 24)

SHRINKAGE PERCENTAGES
$\frac{\text{Gauge Before Felting}}{\text{Gauge After Felting}}$ x 100% = Percentage of Shrinkage

Example (using worsted weight yarn):

Stitch Gauge:	Row Gauge:
$\frac{20}{22.5}$ x 100 = 88%	$\frac{26}{33}$ x 100 = 79%

These are the percentages of shrinkage that must occur during the felting of the knitted sample in order to obtain the correct finished size.
The felted sample should be 88% of the width and 79% of the length of the knitted sample before felting.

Bottle Bag Chart

Yarn Weight	*Sport*	*Worsted*	*Bulky*
No. of Balls SMALL (LARGE)	2 (2) (1¾oz/50g) each approx (164yd/150m)	2 (2) (1¾oz/50g) each approx (114yd/104m)	1 (2) (3½oz/100g) each approx (120yd/110m)
Needle Size (suggested)	3.75mm (CAN9/US5)	4.5mm (CAN7/US7)	6mm (CAN4/US10)
Knitting Gauge	24 sts x 30 rows	20 sts x 26 rows	14 sts x 20 rows
Shrinkage %: (approximate) *WIDTH* *LENGTH*	80% 70%	88% 79%	86% 82%
Work in st st ... SIDE SECTION Small Bag Large Bag BOTTOM SECTION Small Bag Large Bag	60 sts x 138 rows 92 sts x 138 rows 40 sts x 58 rows 40 sts x 58 rows	46 sts x 106 rows 68 sts x 106 rows 30 sts x 44 rows 30 sts x 44 rows	34 sts x 78 rows 50 sts x 78 rows 22 sts x 32 rows 22 sts x 32 rows
Felted Size (WIDTH X LENGTH) SIDE SECTION Small Bag Large Bag BOTTOM SECTION Small Bag Large Bag	(8 x 12½)" (20 x 32)cm (12 x 12½)" (30 x 32)cm (5 x 5)" (13 x 13)cm (5 x 5)" (13 x 13)cm	(8 x 12½)" (20 x 32)cm (12 x 12½)" (30 x 32)cm (5 x 5)" (13 x 13)cm (5 x 5)" (13 x 13)cm	(8 x 12½)" (20 x 32)cm (12 x 12½)" (30 x 32)cm (5 x 5)" (13 x 13)cm (5 x 5)" (13 x 13)cm

INSTRUCTIONS

1. Follow the Bottle Bag Chart (page 86) and knit one side and one bottom section. If knitting the side section in stripe pattern, change yarn color every 4 rows.
2. Felt the knitted pieces to obtain felted measurements.
3. From the smaller felted piece, cut out a circle 4" (10cm) in diameter.
4. Eyelet Openings: On side section, with a long machine stitch or hand basting and MC thread, stitch a line 3" (8cm) below and parallel to top edge (Fig. 4.2). Stitch a second line 1½" (4cm) below and parallel to first stitched line. From center front to each edge, cut 8 openings every ¾" (20mm) between stitched lines (Fig. 4.2). With rotary cutter and "wave" blade, cut along top edge to create decorative finish.
5. With RS together and a flat seam, join side seam of bag and join bottom circular felted piece around lower edge of side felted piece. Turn bag to RS. Beginning at first eyelet opening on one side of center front marking, weave ribbon through eyelets ending at last eyelet before center front. Tie ribbon in bow.

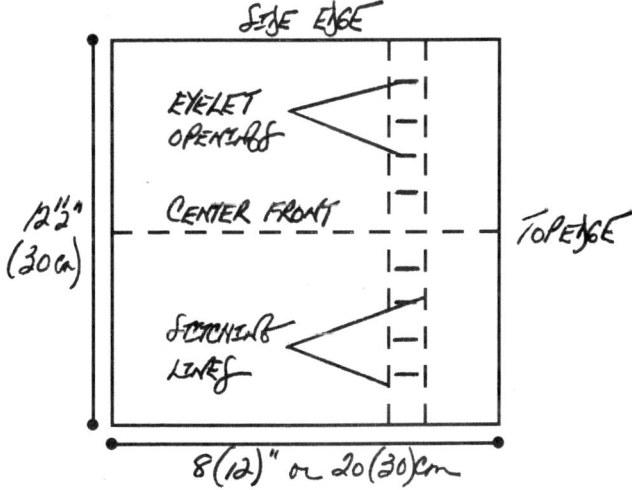

Fig. 4.2 Bottle Bag/Eyelet Placement Guide

Gift Bags

SIZES

Instructions are given for the small size, with the medium and large sizes in parentheses. If one instruction is given, it applies to all sizes.
Small (Medium, Large)

FINISHED SIZES

The finished size is the measurement after felting the knitted pieces and assembly of the bag.
Finished size (width x height)

Small	Medium	Large
(4 x 4)"	(6 x 6)"	(8 x 8)"
(10 x 10)cm	(15 x 15)cm	(20 x 20)cm

MATERIALS

The yarn amounts listed the Gift Bag Chart (see page 89) are what you will need, in a selected yarn weight of 100% animal fiber, to complete one gift bag. If knitting the medium size bag in stripe pattern, choose lengths of yarn in complementary colors of matching yarn weights.

Refer to Bottle Bag Chart for suggested needle size, knitting gauge and shrinkage percentages for the yarn you have chosen.

In addition, you will need:

1 No. 14 "sharp" yarn needle

Sewing thread to match MC and/or invisible nylon thread

Small size: 1 skein (each approx 8¾yd/8m) gold metallic embroidery floss; length of CC yarn for whip stitch trim

Medium size: 1yd (.95m) gold color decorative cording, ¼" (7mm) wide; 1 skein (each approx 8¾yd/8m) gold metallic embroidery floss

Large size: 1yd (.95m) decorative ribbon, 1½" (4cm) wide; length of CC yarn for "lattice" embroidery

GAUGE

Knit a large sample, in the yarn weight you have chosen, at least 8" (20cm) square, to test both knitting gauge and felting shrinkage, as listed in the Bottle Bag Chart.

(See Knitting Your Sample, page 13 and Felting Your Knitted Sample, page 24)

SHRINKAGE PERCENTAGES

$\dfrac{\text{Gauge Before Felting}}{\text{Gauge After Felting}}$ x 100% = Percentage of Shrinkage

Example (using worsted weight yarn):

Stitch Gauge: Row Gauge:

$\dfrac{20}{22.5}$ x 100 = 88% $\dfrac{26}{33}$ x 100 = 79%

These are the percentages of shrinkage that must occur during the felting of the knitted sample in order to obtain the correct finished size.

The felted sample should be 88% of the width and 79% of the length of the knitted sample before felting.

Gift Bag Chart

Yarn Weight	*Sport*	*Worsted*	*Bulky*
No. of Balls Small (Medium, Large)	½ (1, 2) (1¾oz/50g) each approx (164yd/150m)	½ (1, 2) (1¾oz/50g) each approx (114yd/104m)	½ (1, 2) (3½oz/100g) each approx (120yd/110m)
Work in st st ... Small	32 sts x 42 rows	24 sts x 34 rows	22 sts x 24 rows
Medium	46 sts x 66 rows	34 sts x 48 rows	26 sts x 36 rows
Large	60 sts x 88 rows	46 sts x 68 rows	32 sts x 50 rows
Felted Size (WIDTH X LENGTH) Small	(4 x 4)" (10 x 10)om	(4 x 4)" (10 x 10)cm	(4 x 4)" (10 x 10)cm
Medium	(6 x 6)" (15 x 15)cm	(6 x 6)" (15 x 15)cm	(6 x 6)" (15 x 15)cm
Large	(8 x 8)" (20 x 20)cm	(8 x 8)" (20 x 20)cm	(8 x 8)" (20 x 20)cm

INSTRUCTIONS

1. Follow the Gift Bag Chart (page 89) and knit *three* pieces for the selected size. For medium size bag, if knitting stripe pattern, on two pieces change yarn color every:
   Sport ... 22 rows   *Worsted* ... 16 rows   *Bulky* ... 12 rows

2. Felt the knitted pieces to obtain felted measurements.

3. Cut one felted piece into three sections, each measuring: Small size, (1 1/3 x 4)" or (3.3 x 10)cm, medium size, (2 x 6)" or (5 x 15)cm, large size, (2 2/3 x 8)" or (7 x 20)cm. With RS together and a flat seam, join these sections along two short edges to create one length for side/bottom panel.

4. Large Bag: On RS of front and back section, with MC thread and a long machine stitch or hand basting, stitch lines A to B and C to D (Fig. 4.3, page 91). Continue to stitch lines parallel to first lines, 1" (2.5cm) apart. With CC yarn, work a 1" (2.5cm) back stitch (one stitch on each side of a "lattice" square) along all stitched lines.

5. **Assembly**
   Small Bag: With WS together and CC yarn, join side/bottom panel to front and back panels with whip stitch (see an Embroidery Primer, page 32). Whip stitch top edge of bag.
   Medium Bag: With WS together and gold metallic embroidery floss, join side/bottom panel to front and back panels with whip stitch. Whip stitch top edge of bag.
   Large Bag: With RS together, MC yarn and a flat seam, join side/bottom panel to front and back panel with a flat seam. Turn bag to RS.

6. **Finishing**
   Small Bag: Make two small buttonholes centered on each side of bag, 1" (2.5cm) below top edge. Reinforce buttonholes with a grommet or stitching. With embroidery floss, make a 2" (5cm) length tassel (see Tassels, page 36). Fold 10" (25cm) of decorative cord in half and join raw ends to top of tassel. Thread folded end of cord through buttonhole and loop tassel through cord.
   Medium Bag: Make two small buttonholes on each side of bag 1" (2.5cm) below top edge and 1½" (4cm) from each side edge. Reinforce buttonholes with a grommet or stitching. Thread

two lengths of decorative cord through buttonholes and knot. Large Bag: Make two small buttonholes on each side of bag, 1" (2.5cm) below top edge and 1½" (4cm) from each side edge, being careful to center buttonholes within embroidered stitching. Reinforce buttonholes with a grommet or stitching. Thread ribbon through buttonholes and tie into bow.

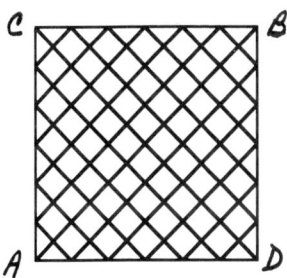

Fig. 4.3 Medium Bag/Lattice Pattern

Felted Sachets

Handknitting that has been felted creates a fabric suitable to hold fragrant potpourri, which can be both pleasing and practical. (See page 75)

Fill these sachets with cedar shavings that have been sprinkled with an aromatic essential oil of cedar or clove. Tuck these sachets among woolen garments and leave them sitting pretty to protect handknit items from unwanted pests.

FINISHED SIZE

The finished size is the measurement __after__ felting the knitted pieces and assembly of the sachet.

One Size

(4½ x 4½)" or (11 x 11)cm

MATERIALS

The yarn amounts listed the Felted Sachet Chart (see page 93) are what you will need, in a selected yarn weight of 100% animal fiber, to complete one sachet.

In addition, you will need:
1 No. 14 "sharp" yarn needle
Sewing thread to match MC
Cedar shavings or potpourri
Essential oil of cedar or clove (optional, to enhance aroma)

GAUGE

Knit a large sample, in the yarn weight you have chosen, at least 8" (20cm) square, to test both knitting gauge and felting shrinkage, as listed in the Felted Sachet Chart.
(See Knitting Your Sample, page 13 and Felting Your Knitted Sample, page 24)

SHRINKAGE PERCENTAGES

$$\frac{\text{Gauge Before Felting}}{\text{Gauge After Felting}} \quad x \quad 100\% \quad = \quad \text{Percentage of Shrinkage}$$

Example (using worsted weight yarn):

Stitch Gauge: Row Gauge:

$\frac{20}{22.5} \quad x \quad 100 \quad = \quad 88\%$ $\frac{26}{33} \quad x \quad 100 \quad = \quad 79\%$

These are the percentages of shrinkage that must occur during the felting of the knitted sample in order to obtain the correct finished size.

The felted sample should be 88% of the width and 79% of the length of the knitted sample before felting.

INSTRUCTIONS

1. Follow the Felted Sachet Chart (page 93) and knit *two* pieces for each sachet.
2. Felt the knitted pieces to obtain felted measurements.
3. Square Sachet: With WS together and MC thread, stitch (with a long machine stitch or hand basting) two felted pieces around three sides, ½" (12mm) from edges. Fill the sachet with potpourri or cedar shavings. Stitch edge closed. With CC yarn, work blanket stitch (See An Embroidery Primer, page 32) around all edges through both thicknesses.
4. Star, Heart and Butterfly Sachets: Enlarge the sachet motif

(continued on page 93)

Felted Sachet Chart

Yarn Weight	*Sport*	*Worsted*	*Bulky*
No. of Balls (MC)	1 (1¾oz/50g) each approx (164yd/150m)	1 (1¾oz/50g) each approx (114yd/104m)	½ (3½oz/100g) each approx (120yd/110m)
Needle Size (suggested)	3.75mm (CAN9/US5)	4.5mm (CAN7/US7)	6mm (CAN4/US10)
Knitting Gauge	24 sts x 30 rows	20 sts x 26 rows	14 sts x 20 rows
Shrinkage %: (approximate) WIDTH LENGTH	80% 70%	88% 79%	86% 82%
Work in st st ...	40 sts x 56 rows	30 sts x 44 rows	22 sts x 30 rows
Felted Size (WIDTH X LENGTH)	(5 x 5)" (13 x 13)cm	(5 x 5)" (13 x 13)cm	(5 x 5)" (13 x 13)cm

(continued from page 92)

patterns (Fig. 4.4, page 94) until grid squares measure 1" (2.5cm). Trace onto heavy paper and cut out to make templates. Cut out two sides of sachet from the felted pieces. With WS together and MC yarn, join edges of sachet with an overcast stitch leaving a 2" (5cm) opening. Fill sachet with potpourri or cedar shavings. Stitch opening closed. With MC yarn, make a 20" (51cm) length of twisted cord, (See Making A Twisted Cord, page 33). Join cord to top of sachet.

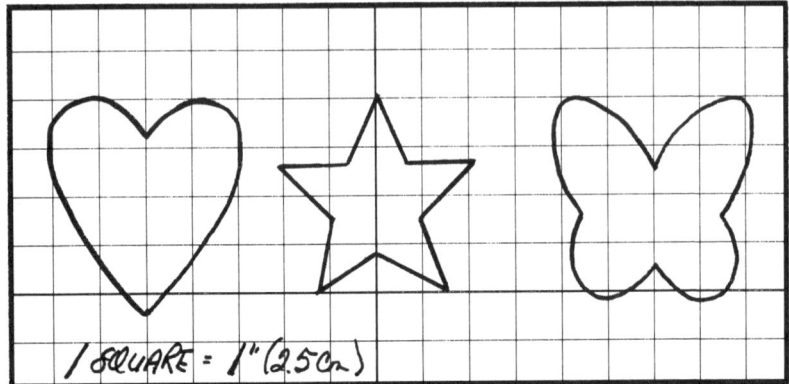

/ SQUARE = 1" (2.5Cm)

Fig. 4.4 Sachet Motif Patterns

Felted Cases and Purses

Felted handknitting makes an ideal soft fabric in which to place special items you want to protect from a scratch or a scrape. The eyeglasses case and the two sizes of envelope purses will provide a gentle covering for practical objects and special treasures. (See page 75)

FINISHED SIZES

The finished size is the measurement after felting the knitted pieces and assembly of the closed case or purse.

Finished Size (width x length)

Eyeglasses Case	Small Purse	Large Purse
(4 x 8)"	(4 x 4)"	(6 x 4¾)"
(10 x 20)cm	(10 x 10)cm	(15 x 12)cm

MATERIALS

The yarn amounts listed in the Felted Cases/Purses Chart (see page 96) are what you will need, in a selected yarn weight of 100% animal fiber, to complete the case or purse. Lengths of yarn (approx 25yd/23m) in two CC are required to complete the motif section. In addition, you will need:

1 No. 14 "sharp" yarn needle
1 snap fastener

GAUGE

Knit a large sample, in the yarn weight you have chosen, at least 8" (20cm) square, to test both knitting gauge and felting shrinkage, as listed in the Felted Cases/Purses Chart.

(See Knitting Your Sample, page 13 and Felting Your Knitted Sample, page 24)

SHRINKAGE PERCENTAGES

Gauge Before Felting   x   100%   =   Percentage of Shrinkage
Gauge After Felting

Example (using worsted weight yarn):

Stitch Gauge:					Row Gauge:				
$\underline{20}$	x	100	=	88%	$\underline{26}$	x	100	=	79%
22.5					33				

These are the percentages of shrinkage that must occur during the felting of the knitted sample in order to obtain the correct finished size.

The felted sample should be 88% of the width and 79% of the length of the knitted sample before felting.

INSTRUCTIONS

1. Follow the Felted Cases/Purses Chart (page 96) and knit a front and a back/flap section in MC, and *two* motif sections, each in one of two CC.

2. Felt the knitted pieces to obtain felted measurements.

3. Enlarge the Cases/Purses Motif Patterns (Fig. 4.5, page 96) until grid squares measure 1" (2.5cm). Trace these patterns onto heavy paper and cut out to make templates. Cut out one motif from each CC felted piece. With WS together (centering the smaller motif on top of the larger), join with CC yarn and whip stitch (See An Embroidery Primer, page 32) around all edges of small motif. Center WS of assembled motif onto RS of flap, matching edges (Fig. 4.6, page 97). With CC yarn and whip stitch, join motif to flap, continuing whip stitch around all edges of motif. With WS together and edges even, join back/flap section to front with CC yarn and whip stitch around all edges.

4. Join snap fastener to WS of assembled motif section.

Felted Cases/Purses Chart

Yarn Weight	*Sport*	*Worsted*	*Bulky*
No. of Balls(MC) EYEGLASSES CASE (SMALL PURSE, LARGE PURSE)	1 (1,1) (1¾oz/50g) each approx (164yd/150m)	1 (1,1) (1¾oz/50g) each approx (114yd/104m)	1 (½, 1) (3½oz/100g) each approx (120yd/110m)
Needle Size (suggested)	3.75mm (CAN9/US5)	4.5mm (CAN7/US7)	6mm (CAN4/US10)
Knitting Gauge	24 sts x 30 rows	20 sts x 26 rows	14 sts x 20 rows
Shrinkage %: (approximate) *WIDTH* *LENGTH*	 80% 70%	 88% 79%	 86% 82%
Work in st st ... FRONT SECTION Eyeglasses Case Small Purse Large Purse	 32 sts x 88 rows 32 sts x 46 rows 42 sts x 48 rows	 24 sts x 66 rows 24 sts x 34 rows 34 sts x 42 rows	 17 sts x 50 rows 17 sts x 24 rows 26 sts x 30 rows
BACK/FLAP SECTION Eyeglasses Case Small Purse Large Purse	 32 sts x 126 rows 32 sts x 82 rows 42 sts x 90 rows	 24 sts x 96 rows 24 sts x 62 rows 34 sts x 70 rows	 17 sts x 72 rows 17 sts x 46 rows 26 sts x 52 rows
MOTIF SECTIONS (2)	40 sts x 58 rows	30 sts x 44 rows	22 sts x 32 rows

(continued on page 97)

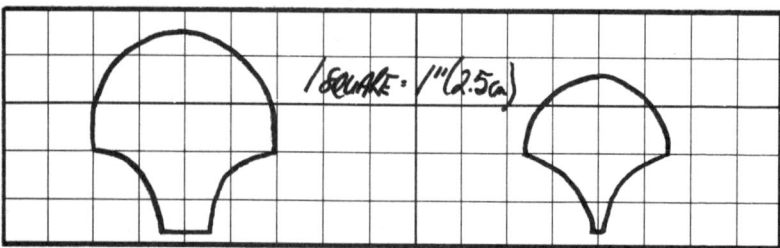

/SQUARE = /"(2.5cm)

Fig. 4.5 Cases/Purses Motif Patterns

(continued from page 96)

Felted Size (WIDTH X LENGTH) FRONT SECTION			
Eyeglasses Case	(4 x 8)" (10 x 20)cm	(4 x 8)" (10 x 20)cm	(4 x 8)" (10 x 20)cm
Small Purse	(4 x 4)" (10 x 10)cm	(4 x 4)" (10 x 10)cm	(4 x 4)" (10 x 10)cm
Large Purse	(6 x 4¾)" (15 x 12)cm	(6 x 4¾)" (15 x 12)cm	(6 x 4¾)" (15 x 12)cm
BACK/FLAP SECTION Eyeglasses Case	(4 x 11½)" (10 x 29)cm	(4 x 11½)" (10 x 29)cm	(4 x 11½)" (10 x 29)cm
Small Purse	(4 x 7½)" (10 x 19)cm	(4 x 7½)" (10 x 19)cm	(4 x 7½)" (10 x 19)cm
Large Purse	(6 x 8¼)" (15 x 21)cm	(6 x 8¼)" (15 x 21)cm	(6 x 8¼)" (15 x 21)cm
MOTIF SECTIONS (each section)	(5 x 5)" (13 x 13)cm	(5 x 5)" (13 x 13)cm	(5 x 5)" (13 x 13)cm

Fig. 4.6 Cases/Purses Motif Placement

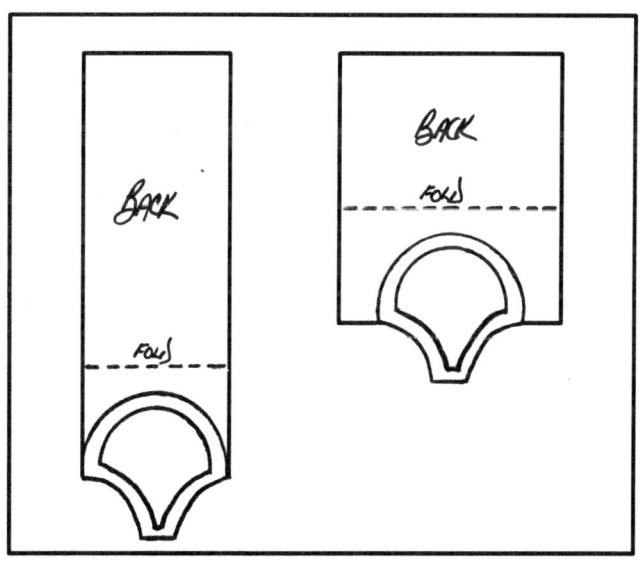

Eyeglasses Case/Small Purse   **Large Purse**

Felted Bookmarks

These are a simple gift item to make, which will give you an opportunity to use any leftover pieces of felting that have accumulated from your project-making. If you do not have any remnant pieces, you can easily knit a piece or two in various colors and yarn weights. Felt these pieces and cut out the simple rectangular shape with decorative blades, add a satin cord and brush the ends into a tassel.

FINISHED SIZE (width x length)
(1½ x 6½)" or (4 x 16) cm

MATERIALS
Lengths of yarn of 100% animal fiber
In addition you will need:
Sewing thread
Rotary blade, with decorative "wave" or "pinking" blade
Lengths of embroidery floss
Purchased satin cord or yarn twisted cord (See Making a Twisted Cord, page 33)

INSTRUCTIONS
1. Knit in stocking (stockinette) st:
    Sport - 16 sts x 86 rows
    Worsted - 12 sts x 66 rows
    Bulky - 8 sts x 48 rows
2. Felt the knitted pieces. From a piece of heavy paper, cut out a template of (1½ x 6½)" or (4 x 16)cm.
3. Using the template, cut out bookmarks from the felted pieces with a rotary cutter and decorative "pinking" or "wave" blade *or* if using felting remnants, piece remnants together in a patchwork arrangement and use the template to cut out a bookmark from the patchworked piece, finishing seams with cross stitch or whip stitch (see An Embroidery Primer, page 32).
4. Turn ½" (12mm) at top of each bookmark to WS, enclosing a 6" (15cm) length of cord.   Tie cord in a knot and brush ends to form a tassel.

Mail Order Shopping Guide

ELANN FIBRE
Stocks Brown Sheep Naturespun (100% wool) available in sport and worsted weights and Brown Sheep Lamb's Pride (85% wool /15% mohair) in worsted and bulky weights. Shipping available within Canada and U.S.A. Catalog available.

Mailing Addresses:

Box 771	Box 257
Cranbrook, BC	Eureka, MT 59917-0257
Canada	U.S.A.
V1C 4J5	

Order Line: 1-800-720-0616
Fax: 1-250-426-0618/1-888-252-0618
E/Mail: elann@cyberlink.bc.ca
Elann Web Site: http://www.elann.com

HERRSCHNERS
Stocks Paton's Classic Wool (100% wool) worsted weight yarn in a shade range of over 30 colors.   Catalog available.

Mailing Address:
2800 Hoover
Stevens Point, WI 54481
U.S.A.
Order Line: 1-800-441-0838
Herrschners Web Site: http://www.herschners.com

RAM WOOLS

Stocks Paton's Classic Wool (100% wool) worsted weight yarn and Lopi (100% wool) in worsted and bulky weights. Shipping available within Canada and U.S.A. Catalog available.

Mailing Address:
143 Smith Street
Winnipeg, MB
Canada
R3C 1J5
Order Line: 1-800-263-8002
E/Mail: ram@gaspard.ca
Ram Wools Web Site: http://www.gaspard.ca

Index

Workbook Page

Yarn: _____   Color name: _____

Color No: _____   Dye lot: _____

Sample knit: _____ sts x _____ rows   Needle size: _____

Gauge (before felting): _____ sts x _____ rows to 4" (10cm)

KNITTED SAMPLE MEASUREMENTS

" (cm) width   " (cm) width

" (cm)   " (cm)
length   length

Before Felting   After Felting

Felting method used: _____

Time: _____

Gauge (after felting): _____ sts x _____ rows to 4" (10cm)

Percentage of shrinkage:
(Before Felting Gauge x 100 ÷ After Felting Gauge = Percentage of Shrinkage)

Stitch Gauge: _____ x 100 ÷ _____ = _____ %

Row Gauge: _____ x 100 ÷ _____ = _____ %

Workbook Page

Yarn: _____   Color name: _____

Color No: _____   Dye lot: _____

Sample knit: _____ sts x _____ rows   Needle size: _____

Gauge (before felting): _____ sts x _____ rows to 4" (10cm)

KNITTED SAMPLE MEASUREMENTS

" (cm) width   " (cm) width

" (cm) length   "(cm) length

Before Felting   After Felting

Felting method used: _____

Time: _____

Gauge (after felting): _____ sts x _____ rows to 4" (10cm)

Percentage of shrinkage:
(Before Felting Gauge x 100 ÷ After Felting Gauge = Percentage of Shrinkage)

Stitch Gauge: _____ x 100   ÷   _____ = _____ %

Row Gauge: _____ x 100   ÷   _____ = _____ %

Workbook Page

Yarn: _____   Color name: _____

Color No: _____   Dye lot: _____

Sample knit: _____ sts x _____ rows   Needle size: _____

Gauge(before felting): _____ sts x _____ rows to 4" (10cm)

KNITTED SAMPLE MEASUREMENTS

" (cm) width   " (cm) width

" (cm)   "(cm)
length   length

Before Felting   After Felting

Felting method used: _____

Time: _____

Gauge(after felting): _____ sts x _____ rows to 4" (10cm)

Percentage of shrinkage:
(Before Felting Gauge x 100 ÷ After Felting Gauge = Percentage of Shrinkage)

Stitch Gauge: _____ x 100 ÷ _____ = _____ %

Row Gauge: _____ x 100 ÷ _____ = _____ %

Workbook Page

Yarn: _____   Color name: _____

Color No: _____   Dye lot: _____

Sample knit: _____ sts x _____ rows   Needle size: _____

Gauge(before felting): _____ sts x _____ rows to 4" (10cm)

KNITTED SAMPLE MEASUREMENTS

" (cm) width   " (cm) width

" (cm)   "(cm)
length   length

Before Felting   After Felting

Felting method used: _____

Time: _____

Gauge(after felting): _____ sts x _____ rows to 4" (10cm)

Percentage of shrinkage:
(Before Felting Gauge x 100 ÷ After Felting Gauge = Percentage of Shrinkage)

Stitch Gauge: _____ x 100   ÷   _____   = _____ %

Row Gauge: _____ x 100   ÷   _____   = _____ %